The Leadership Tinderbox
Coaching to Kindle the Passion for Success

Barbara Wichman

Address all author inquiries to:
Barbara Wichman
barbara@barbarawichman.com
barbarawichman.com
Every attempt has been made to source all information properly.

Author Photos by Becky Mokelke Photography

ISBN-13: 978-1-7336012-0-7
eBook ISBN 978-1-7336012-1-4
Barbara Wichman

This book is dedicated to Rebecca, my daughter, the light of my soul.

And to my mom, who is always by my side.

CONTENTS

INTRODUCTION

I am lucky. I am one of those people who has never thought of my job as a job. I have always loved what I do. When people ask me about retirement, I start laughing. Why on earth would I stop doing what I love to do, to sit around and try to find things to do all day? I have yet to lose the burning curiosity of my profession. I am so grateful for that.

Throughout my career I had mentors. One of my mentors challenged me to write a book, a book with an HR perspective. I never forgot about his challenge. However, I did allow other priorities to get in my way.

One sunny day, as I was sitting out on my patio working on another book, that challenge came back to me in full force with this thought, "I wonder how HR professionals see leaders?" I could see my mentor sitting across the table from me saying, "You should write a book from an HR perspective." That sunny day on the patio, I decided to take on the challenge.

This book is not theoretical.

This book is not fictional.

The Leadership Tinderbox shares real-life stories and lessons on leadership through the eyes of human resource (HR) professionals. The very function of the HR role provides a multifaceted perspective on leaders. HR holds a more multi-directional lens on leaders than anyone else in the organization. They receive input on the leader from employees, managers, leaders, other HR professionals, clients, consultants, assessments, feedback tools, performance management, succession processes, and from the leaders themselves. HR sees all.

That is the value of looking at leadership through the eyes of HR. They have a perspective on leaders that is robust and incredibly significant.

This book is the result of interviewing HR professionals about leadership. I set forth on this journey to understand how they saw leadership through their multifaceted HR lens. Because they are the ones to see so much, I was curious as to what stood out for them. Patterns emerged that HR leaders have seen over time, in different industries, different functions, all leadership levels. There were patterns of success and patterns of failure.

WHY IT MATTERS

Year after year, Gallup Polls continue to show that over 65 percent of employees are disengaged. The 2017 Gallup Poll revealed that 51 percent of employees are looking for a new job or watching for new job opportunities. Something is not right in the workplace. It starts with leadership. How many times have you heard, "**people leave leaders, not jobs**." The challenge with employee disengagement is not an anomaly. It is an epidemic.

WHO BENEFITS FROM READING
THE LEADERSHIP TINDERBOX

If you are an HR leader, this book offers food for thought as you support your business leaders. If you are a new leader, this might be the golden handbook you always wanted. If you are a leader who is struggling, the lessons in this book might help identify where and why you are struggling, and ideas for actions to take to recover with a positive outcome. If you are a great leader, there are some messages to consider and share, no matter how long you have held your title.

BEFORE YOU READ THIS BOOK

Because the stories and examples shared by the interviewees are true stories, there was a need to alter some of the specifics to protect those that are represented in the stories. For example, the subject of a story may be a male, however the story may portray them as a female. Any details that caused a person or place to be easily identified have been removed or changed. The stories are true and real. Some of the details are changed.

You may see a line of words in quotes as if these were the exact words spoken. They are not. They are paraphrased based on recollections. The stories are real-life experiences shared in story form with the intent to share the point and the resulting impact, as well as maintaining the privacy of those in the stories.

My agreement with the HR leaders, who were from large and primarily global companies, was that I would not share their names, the names of the people, or the names of the companies. I made that agreement because the stories they shared are intense. And raw. And brutal. And funny. And touching. And at times, made me gasp. Some stories were so disturbing, I chose only to share the highlights and not the details.

Each story provided insight into the world of leadership.

ABOUT CHAPTER TWO

The content of chapter two is the result of asking this question:

Who is the leader you admire the most and why?

Chapter Two is all about the HR leader's experiences - the leader THEY admire the most. The remaining chapters share their stories and thoughts on leadership—and not just HR leadership — with all leadership.

I KNOW WHO

I want to offer one more point before you read this book. If we were to sit down with a group of HR professionals, or any leaders for that matter, one might tell a story, and at least three people at the table will say, "I have a story just like that!" Then we will all agree, "I can't believe more than one person in the world did that."

What am I trying to say? If you read a story and think, "I know exactly who that is!" Probably not. There are so many stories that will have elements of similar situations, it is probable that you know of a similar one.

CHAPTER ONE
BOYS ARE PRESIDENTS

THE BIG DAY

Waiting to run out to the playground was the best anticipation and today was no different. Afternoon recess was my favorite. I was always looking forward to stretching my legs. It had been a long day in this sixth-grade class. After all, I had prepared posters and a speech in preparation for the big vote, the vote for Class President. It was my first run for office. I had no idea if I had any chance of winning, but I knew I wanted to give it a try. My friends were encouraging, so I was feeling good about a possible win.

I was nervous and frankly a little scared. I was competitive in sports, playground games, and school activities. I was not particularly eager to lose. And losing this, it would be very different. It would be public humiliation. But I had to try. I did not want to give up because I was afraid of losing.

Recess provided a big boost in my confidence. Many of my classmates came up to me to tell me they had voted for me. With each person telling me I was their presidential choice, my excitement grew a bit more. Maybe I could win?

When recess was over, I ran back to the room with all my friends. The results of the vote were going to be announced. I sat down and nervously flipped open the top of my desk. I wanted to grab a pencil and some paper in case I needed to take notes. I didn't know what notes I might take. It really was something to do to channel my nervous energy until I knew the results of the vote.

The teacher came to the front of the room to announce the winner. "Our Class President is…" she paused.

"Michael!"

Dead silence.

Michael? Really? How can that be?

I was devastated.

I heard a classmate shout, "No way." I looked at my friend sitting next to me. She said, "I don't believe it." I looked around the room, and it felt like everyone was looking at me. I don't know if they were or were not, but I felt like all eyes were on me. Were they waiting for a reaction? A protest? I gave them nothing. I sat in silence. My face probably turned red, but I did not say a word.

Michael? Really? I was genuinely devastated and embarrassed. I knew I should never have gotten my hopes up. The teacher spoke up and said, "Congratulations Michael. You are our new Class President." The class was silent.

I managed to finish out the day without too much drama. But I was hurting inside. I did not cry. I was quiet. I did not want to talk about it.

At the end of the day, the teacher asked me to stay after school for a few minutes. Once everyone left, she shut the big wooden door with the huge glass window and she sat next to me. She looked me in the eyes. I may have forgotten exactly what she said, however I clearly remember the message.

"I know you are upset. I can see it on your face. I want to be honest with you. You received most of the votes — almost all of them. However, this vote is for Class President. Girls aren't presidents, boys are. So, Michael had to be the president because he is a boy. Hopefully you feel better because you know you would have been president based on the votes."

Feel better? I was stunned into silence. I don't remember what I said or if I said anything at all. All I knew was what she told me did not make me feel better. It was like a second loss on top of the first one. Now, in addition falsely losing the Class President vote, I was a loser because I was a girl. I was more hurt than before. I never told my mom or my dad. It was a loss in which I suffered in silence. It was my first lesson in leadership.

My lessons from that day:

- Girls are not leaders (which I overcame).
- Only boys are leaders (which was the societal norm at the time).
- My leader, the teacher, could make bad choices based on her beliefs (following societal norms).
- Leaders have the power to influence those around them in many ways, including causing emotional, psychological, and spiritual pain (the teacher's intentions did not have the soothing impact she had hoped).

Something happened to my teacher that night. I have no idea what it was. Perhaps her conscience? The next day started as usual and then she asked for our attention. She told us that because of some rule, we would not have a Class President.

The lessons from day two held these learnings:

- Leaders would rather lie than be honest about their poor decisions.
- Leaders will use excuses to mask their mistakes.
- The new decision could be just as stupid as the first decision.
- Guilt has power.

My second day of lessons about leadership were just as powerful as the first day lessons.

We all have lessons from our experiences with leaders. The hope is that the lessons are positive. These lessons stay with us for a long time, sometimes a lifetime. Unless more experiences can negate the first lesson, life's trajectory could be negatively impacted. I was lucky. I had many more experiences that put me in leadership roles that allowed me to overcome the impact of those first lessons.

The lessons from the Class President experience stayed with me for a lifetime. I recently told my mom about the class vote. She was angry. She could not believe that teacher, who was so well respected, would have made such terrible decisions. She wondered why I did not tell her. After all, she always had my back and still does.

My sixth-grade teacher might have been nervous as she wondered what I told my mom that night. After all, there was history with my mom and the teachers at that school. In third grade, I kicked Tim in the shins which sent him crying to the teacher. I was sent to the principal's office. Tim teased me relentlessly because I wore saddle shoes. Finally, one day I came home mad as could be. I was tired of the relentless teasing day after day. My mom said if Tim teased me again, I was supposed to kick him in the shins with my saddle shoes as hard as I could.

The next day was no different. The teasing began while we were at morning recess. I did exactly as my mom told me. I kicked Tim in the shins as hard as I could with my super heavy saddle shoes. The teacher called my mom to tell her I had done this terrible deed. My mom responded, "Good. I told her to kick him in the shins!" The teacher responded. "Mrs. B., you scare me." My mom hung up the phone.

Maybe my sixth-grade teacher thought she better think of something before she received a call from my mom. I will never know. However, that Class President vote provided me with my first lessons in leadership.

And let's not forget poor Michael. It was probably not his favorite memory on leadership either.

WHO WANTS STEVE?

Lessons on leadership start early in our lives. Think about it. On the playground there are those children that are organizing games, making decisions about rules, and directing other kids as to their roles in the games. When it comes time to choose teams, a leader is expected to put together a winning team. That is where some of the first lessons about being valued are learned.

Whether it is recess, backyard games, or organized school physical education classes, the process to choose teams is often the same. The team leaders are self-selected or chosen by the teacher. Once the leaders are selected, the rest of the kids line up, and the leaders take turns picking players for their team. The first ones chosen are usually friends of the leader, the loyalty factor. Then the kids known to be good athletes, or good at the game, are selected. Oh yes, eventually all are chosen to be on the team, but not until after the apprehension and embarrassment of being picked last has reared its ugly head.

"Who is going to take Steve?"

Steve was often the last one chosen for the team. He loved to play sports and always looked forward to being on the team. He had to endure the discomfort of being picked last for a few minutes each time the teams were selected. As Steve explained, once he was on the team, the uncomfortable feeling went away because now he was a part of the team.

After the teams are selected, the leader has a new role which is to focus and engage everyone in playing to win. The collective focus is now on winning the game. Everyone on the team has a role to play. Now the entire team has responsibility for everyone to be supported to win the game.

Whether Steve was chosen first or last, each great play resulted in kudos. Each misstep met with acknowledgment of the effort put forth. The team came together with a common focus: To win the game.

Leadership lessons learned on the playground:

- On any team, there are going to be players with various levels of capability.
- Once you have a team, every person has a role.
- Every team member receives support.
- Teams win together and lose together.

The lessons on leadership begin early from the classroom to the playground, and everywhere in between. Leaders are valuable. Leaders matter.

The teaching that the role of leadership is significant begins at a very early age.

- Leaders hold power.
- Leaders have control.
- Leaders can make you feel good or bad about yourself.

We learn that leaders are expected to be extraordinary people. And they are. So is every human being. However, when given the title of leader, expectations for greatness increases.

Young leaders are given power, with no lessons on leadership. Adults are given roles as leaders, often with no lessons on leadership.

All everyone knows is this: Leadership matters.

Do you remember your first lesson in leadership?

CHAPTER TWO

YOUR FIRST LEADER

REMEMBER YOUR FIRST?

I attended a fundraiser and was sitting at a table with six other women. We spent our time over lunch sharing personal stories. The topic of leadership came up as we spoke about recent high school graduates and how they were living through their recent "off to college" transition. Could they maintain the same level of achievement after being successful students and leaders in high school? After all, high school is a pretty controlled environment and typically offers lots of support. College, much less so. Because I was in the middle of writing this book and the topic had eased into leadership, I saw the opportunity to ask the question I have asked of many people, "Who is the leader you admire the most, and why?" A huge smile came across the face of my dear friend Andrea who was sitting next to me. She responded, "My mentor!"

I asked her what her mentor did that made him so admired. Her response was quick. "That's hard to say because we have been friends for many years, ever since he was first my mentor. We share all kinds of information all the time! We talk about everything!" It was easy to see how that friendship blossomed. Andrea is not only exceptionally talented as a surgeon, but also a human being with a huge heart. I could feel the mutual respect they had for one another as she spoke of him.

"My first boss is also someone I would say is my most admired leader. My first real boss," Andrea added.

I wanted to understand more about his influence on her. "Do you remember what he said or how he made you feel?" Her face lit up as she responded, "He believed in me. Because he believed in me, I believed even more in myself." Andrea's response was an example of the potential power and impact of being someone's first leader.

Do you remember your first great teacher?

Your first best friend?

Do you remember your first great leader?

I'm not talking about your first manager, the one who directed you and whose sole focus was getting tasks completed. I'm talking about your first leader. That person who truly cared about you as a person and wanted you to succeed. That person that brings a massive smile to your face, like Andrea. Do remember what your experience was like with that leader? How they made you feel? How they made you think about your own skills and capabilities?

Andrea also shared the downside of belief or lack thereof. She had a college advisor who told her she should think about being a technician, not a surgeon. In his view, she did not have what it would take to be a surgeon. A specialized, orthopedic surgeon nonetheless. She could have let those words change the course of her career and create a permanent frown on her forehead like she had when she spoke about him. That advice was easy for her to walk away from because she had a mentor that genuinely believed in her. However, what if she did not have a mentor to counter that bad advice? Would those narrow beliefs have overpowered her own? Thankfully, that did not happen.

For over half of those interviewed for this book, it was clear that their first leader was the leader whom they admired the most, and the one who influenced them in many ways.

- That first leader held a very special place in their heart.
- That first leader made them feel capable of doing anything.

- That first leader always had time for them.

- The memory of that first leader had their voices utterly full of joy.

A few of those I spoke with started by saying, "You know, I was going to say another person whom I admire. But after really thinking some more, it was my first leader." They were thinking of saying national leaders, social leaders, business leaders, charismatic leaders from history. Yet they came back to their first leader. What was it about that first leader that had such a tremendous impact on them?

Not only did they remember their first leader, they distinctly remember the way that leader made them feel. They had passion in their voices as they shared stories of new and challenging projects, hours of listening to words of encouragement that motivated them to do more and be better. I could hear that smile, that intensity, and that joyful trip down memory lane through their stories. Their stories were full of leaders giving them undivided attention, unbridled belief in their abilities, and unyielding trust.

There were times when that first leader they admired the most was not their direct manager. It was a leader they interacted with during their first job. And in their short time together, that leader conveyed a strong message of confidence.

"INSIDERS AND FIELD"

I knew exactly what they were talking about. I have my own powerful and impassioned memory of my first leader. Oh yes, I had many managers up to that point, but this manager was different. I knew I wanted to work for him as we were progressing through the interview. He was so different, but I could not put my finger on why at the time. Even during the interview, his confidence gave way to building my own confidence.

After starting the job, his enthusiasm for what I was going to do, and his belief that it was going to be remarkable, became my own.

I was beyond motivated. There were times when I worked all night long in a massive and shadow-filled building that was somewhat lonely and a bit frightening in the wee hours. The drive to be better overwhelmed my fear. I was driven to be more than expectations because of my leader's belief in me. This man was a true leader. He also said words one day that have stayed with me for years.

The day is vividly imprinted in my memory. A day where my frustration with a colleague came to a head. This colleague was new to the team and, although he was pleasant, he was difficult to work alongside. His field experience overshadowed those on the team, and he knew it. He had been described as a superstar. His field experience was important for our team's credibility. I understood that, as did all the team members.

Our learning team was composed of the "insiders" and the "field." The "insiders" worked within the corporate walls developing content, supporting the businesses as internal consultants, and providing support to the "field." The "field" worked outside the confines of the corporate walls and supported the field leadership development, consulted with the field business leaders, as well as facilitated courses for the organization, courses developed by the "insiders."

Our team was built on several principles. We valued hard work, respect for each other, challenged each other to do great things, and, maybe most importantly, we were to live the corporate values. We were expected to be role models for the rest of the organization.

The entire team of talented folks came together for a week of learning and team building. The new courses created by the "insiders," were going to be shared with the "field" so they could facilitate the new classes for their clients.

Our newest team member, with his tremendous field experience, was tasked with creating a highly anticipated course for field leaders. There was great excitement for what he had developed. The only problem was his course was unfinished. It was a mess. He was not prepared to share anything. The time came for him to share his unfinished course with the team. I overheard him say to a colleague, "We will just shove it down their throats."

I was incensed.

He was not the person I wanted to work alongside. I stood up from the table and walked out the door of the meeting room. I was extremely frustrated. My leader saw the strain on my face. He pulled me aside to understand what had happened. After all, I loved working on this team and he knew it. What would cause my anger to flare up so sharply?

I was sincere in sharing my frustration. I indicated that I was not sure I wanted to remain on the team with this new colleague. My leader shared the most powerful words he could have chosen at that moment which I remember so vividly.

"Don't ever let anyone else's behavior cause you to make a decision that you will regret later."

That phrase struck me like a rogue pitch in the gut at that very moment. With fantastic detail, I remember the room we sat in as he delivered those words. I remember how he sat. I remember the directness of his eyes as he spoke, making sure that I heard him through my frustration. It was a powerful moment.

The words he chose and how he delivered them were impactful then, and they're still meaningful today. This person was not my first manager. However, he was, without a doubt, my first leader.

YOU CAN'T FAKE IT

My experience with my first leader mirrors that of over half of the HR leaders interviewed. Their first leader had the most significant impact on the belief they held in themselves and became a powerful influence on how they grew and developed as leaders. They recall the profound coaching. They felt the belief those leaders had in them. Those "first" leaders left an indelible mark. What was it about those first-time leaders that caused them to leave such an impression? The responses revolved around three simple phrases.

1. They made me feel like I was the only one who mattered in the room.
2. They gave me their uninterrupted time.
3. They trusted that I could accomplish something before I believed I could do it.

It was clear the admiration held for these first leaders remained present and powerful. There was no question that each of these "first" leaders wanted others to succeed.

Those on the receiving end could feel and hear and see just how much their success was a priority for that leader. One HR leader shared, "There was an absolute trust that she was an advocate for me, and she was not even my direct manager." When was the last time you felt that level of trust? When words and actions aligned consistently?

One story was shared where a leader said, "I want you to be successful." The entire delivery was wrapped with an "I don't care" look in his eyes and tone in their voice. That leader said the words, but there was no passion, no truth behind it. It was an example of a leader doing what they had been coached to say because it is what great leaders do. He could not deliver the phrase with any impact because they did not believe it. You can't fake belief in someone. The lack of authenticity is glaring.

I suspect we have all had those interactions with a leader, a coach, a teacher, or someone else where they say words that are meant to be supportive and you walk away thinking, "That was a waste of words and time." The negative impacts can be as powerful as the positive impacts.

Leaders who are surrounded by first-time employees have people who are sponges. They are anticipating learning and growth. As a leader, it is an incredible opportunity and unbelievable responsibility.

That depth of passion, that honest belief, you know it when it is real. You know when the leaders want it for you. It seems like they feel it more than you do. It is these moments that inspire you. They imprint upon you that you truly matter. You are valued. You are seen.

The amount of time spent between the leader and the employee was secondary to the belief conveyed during their time together.

There is tremendous value in understanding that if you are someone's first leader, you have an opportunity to leave lasting impressions that form beliefs about capabilities for a lifetime. It is a chance to embed in people the feeling that they are valued, they truly matter, and that you trust them. That is a leadership privilege, and an incredible opportunity.

When a leader believes in you and trusts you, sometimes more than you believe yourself, you have a platform to flourish and realize your greatest potential. Is this experience limited to first-time employee/leader relationships? No! However, there was something magical in the stories shared about first leaders. These are the leaders that people will still talk about with passion even 20 or more years later.

"C" TO THE THIRD POWER:
COMMUNICATION, CHARISMA, AND CHARACTER

There are billions of people in the world. There is a good chance not everyone is going to like you, or you like them. As a leader, this is also true. There are a few things you can do to improve your odds of gaining respect and create lasting relationships.

- Barbara Wichman

It was clear that these "first" leaders created an environment of trust, growth, and belief. These leaders left lasting positive impressions and were said to have an "X-Factor." This X-Factor is described as a combination of the three Cs: Communication, charisma, and character. The three Cs represented their ability to connect to the masses as well as with individuals. They used the right combination of words backed with actions, sincerity, and vulnerability.

COMMUNICATION

The capable communicators truly understand what people need to hear in that moment. These powerful communicators are not known as entertaining, nor do they rely on the shock value of profanity or outrageous statements to unbalance the crowd. They have a strong presence and unwavering confidence in their spoken and written word. They communicate their belief in the strength and the capabilities of those listening, whether it is a large group or face-to-face across the conference table. When you have their attention, you have all their attention.

Great communicators also know when to listen. They genuinely understand all facets of communication.

It was the same experience I had with my first true leader. I always enjoyed being in his presence because he made me feel incredible about my work, and he proved to be trustworthy time and time again. I never felt a hidden agenda. He told stories that showed he was vulnerable and perfectly imperfect. He made work fun.

Vulnerability and being authentic in stories allow others to relate to the leader. Leaders openly sharing struggles and challenges show they are human and welcome continuous learning. Creating this type of environment allows for bonding between the leaders and employees in a real and meaningful way. It develops followers. That is what leaders want and need in the end: Followers.

One of the challenges that leaders face is creating a safe environment whereby followers feel comfortable enough to speak up about the positive results and the negative results. More than one decision has been less than stellar because the leader lacked the full story and had limited exposure to the truth of the situation. Employees are often fearful to bring up bad news to leaders. They fear being labeled as "not a team player" because they challenged the status quo and collective decisions. More than one person has been chastised for bringing up a problem, concern, or failure. No one wants to be the bearer of bad news.

One powerful leader encouraged the sharing of good news and managed to mitigate the fear of sharing bad news during his meetings by requiring misses and mistakes to be shared. All his meetings were prepared stand-up meetings, meaning everyone walked into the room ready to share their updates, good and bad. Before they came to the meeting, they were to write three ups and three downs on an index card. Each person had to have an index card. Not a piece of paper. Not notes on their computer. An index card. Each person had to share three ups and three downs. Each person was required to stand during the meeting because it was a "stand-up" meeting. There was no attending without being prepared. There was no kicking back in a chair pretending to pay attention. There was no hemming and hawing around a topic.

The stand-up meetings were intentional.

- **Always come prepared**. There were no excuses allowed.
- **Be concise**. The three ups and three downs must be expressed within the confines of a 3x5 notecard. The person read the card aloud.
- **Pay attention**. Don't expect to come to a meeting and not participate. Be engaged.
- **Stand up**. Who wants to stand up for an hour while someone is pontificating a point that adds little value?
- **Act as a team**. Listen to each other. Support each other.
- **Expect to share problems**. Sharing the three downs was followed with these questions:

    - *Is there anyone in this room that can help you?*

    - *What do you need to solve these problems?*

    - *How can I help you?*

In the beginning, articulation of problems and identifying help was a significant challenge for those attending the meetings. The discomfort of having to share that things were not going well was extremely uncomfortable. Who wanted to walk into a meeting with your boss and peers and share three items that were not going well? It was an unwritten cultural rule. Do not share things that are not going well. Never show weakness. Never show you are not capable of the leadership job.

This leader understood the negative impact of the unwritten rules. He understood how to create an environment where communication was truthful and vulnerable and expected nothing less. He knew how to facilitate dynamic and effective communication processes that supported problem-solving, team collaboration and eliminate the stigma of having to air problems publicly. You could not pry his team apart with a crowbar. The outcome of this approach, among other powerful leadership qualities, created a tight-knit team with outstanding accomplishments.

A leader that is a great communicator knows how to read a room, is present with and respectful of the current environment. Effective leaders are not afraid to try new methods to create compelling communication experiences.

CHARISMA

Charisma is more than being charming. It is the ability to attract and influence those around you. There are specific qualities that enhance charisma. Confidence, passion, being friendly, and welcoming are a few. Those that smile easily and engage others by being present during personal interactions are considered charismatic. Charismatic leaders seem to get along with others easily. They always seem to know when to say the right thing at the moment. Employees are drawn to charismatic leaders.

The most charismatic leader I ever met was Arthur Martinez. He was the CEO of Sears, Roebuck and Co. When he walked into a room, you could feel his presence. You may not have seen him enter the room, but you would feel it. It made everyone stand a little taller and pay closer attention. He was known for saying something that made everyone smile and relax.

Those around him listened more intently for his words of wisdom. He knew he had that effect and used it in a positive way rather than a "greater than thou" approach. He held respect for everyone and made sure they felt it. Have you ever experienced a leader like that? You will never forget a leader with that quality.

What if a leader does not have that natural charisma? After all, not many people have that level of magnetism. One HR leader shared, "Developing strong presentation skills magnifies the connection the leader has with the crowd. It is one way to build a charismatic style even if they are not all that charismatic." Developing presentation skills also helps to develop interpersonal skills.

There are some that are naturally charismatic, like Arthur Martinez. However, any leader can develop charismatic qualities. Showing confidence, having a passion for the work, believing in the future, being genuinely friendly to others, these are qualities leaders can develop. They may need some coaching, but it is indeed possible.

CHARACTER

True character is not always visible right away. Everything can be terrific until something goes wrong. Just one thing… that is all it takes.

What is character? Character is being honest and ethical, having courage and being responsible for decisions and actions. Those with favorable character are loyal in their relationships, even when times are bad. Leaders with good character are role models for those around them.

One executive would walk the halls smiling and greeting others as though the world was his oyster. There were times he would get so riled up when something did not go his way, his face would turn red and veins would pop out on his neck. He would insult and chastise those in his presence. One manager would laugh at his outbursts. For most on the receiving end of his thrashing, his eruptions were emotionally destructive. His tirades intended to demoralize his target. People feared his outbursts.

One day, during one of his tirades, a manager calmly said to him, "You might want to be careful. You look like you are going to have a heart attack. The veins in your neck are sticking out, and your face is all red." There was no reaction to the outburst, just a statement of fact. The leader was not quite sure how to handle the comment. He was used to people cowering in fear. The executive calmed himself when he realized this one person was not going to give him the satisfaction of fear. His bullying was not going to get what he wanted with this manager. He enjoyed the fear he created, and once he could not get it, he stopped. Years later, he died from a heart attack while swimming. The manager was right.

Having strength in character is foundational to respecting others, maintaining balance, and being trustworthy. It is an essential part of being a great leader. People know soon enough if a leader's character is destructive. If your first leader lacks character, it will be hard to regain the trust of leaders after that. You will always be looking for the crack, the reason to not trust.

There are leaders whose behavior reflects their amazing character.

I was employed in my first corporate job for about three weeks and having a great time. One afternoon, I was approached and asked if I would be comfortable helping with the store manager training school. The training was five days long, and there were 40 store managers in attendance. The person in charge of the school had a family emergency. They needed someone to introduce the speakers, ensure everything went smoothly, and support the participants during the week. Of course, I said yes! I was elated to be asked to be a part of such an important event. My manager asked me if I knew how to pronounce the leader's name. Of course, I did. It was easy. I said his name.

Wrong!

Thank goodness my manager asked me. That would have been so embarrassing. Okay, I would be ready. I was going to introduce the CEO at the store manager school. I was honored to be trusted with such an important role. Later that day my manager walked by my cube and stuck his head in, "What's his name?"

Again, I mispronounced his name.

My manager laughed. "You'll be fine."

I vowed to have the correct pronunciation roll off my tongue easily. I was going to imprint the correct pronunciation in my brain so when the time came, my nerves would not get the best of me and cause me to mess it up.

So, I practiced. I repeated the CEO's last name over and over. I repeated his name out loud and in my head.

My manager poked his head into my cubicle and asked me again, "What's his name?"

I said it. Correctly.

"You got it."

I knew I was not going to mess it up.

The day came. Forty new store managers in the audience, waiting for our CEO to arrive and address the group. They were excited, and so was I! We were all anticipating his arrival.

I told the class, "I am going to get started. As soon as the CEO enters the room, I am going to go directly into his introduction, and then we will circle back."

Everyone agreed to the plan. They were so excited to have the CEO address them.

I began reviewing the agenda for the day. I felt him walk in the room. He had that kind of presence. I immediately went into the introduction.

"I would like to introduce the captain of your ship, Mr. Arder…" I immediately threw my head into my hands and these words passed my lips with absolute exasperation at my mistake, "Oh shit. (pause) Arthur."

I looked up and saw forty faces with expressions that could be best described as seeing a horrible car crash. I felt a bead of sweat roll down my temple. I looked off to the left and saw the CEO put his hands in his pockets, shaking his head from side to side, as he walked to the front of the room.

"I can honestly say I have never been introduced like that before."

I walked to the side of the room and sat in my chair. I wanted the floor to open and swallow me. Anything to get me out of that room.

He shared his inspiring messages with the class. When he was done, he turned to me and said, "Thank you." And he left. I was sick to my stomach. I stood up and continued with my review of the agenda and the day went on.

At the end of the day, I walked back to my cubicle and sat down, still reeling from my mistake. My manager walked into my cube with a big smile. "How did it go?"

"It went well. Everyone in the class is very engaged."

"Great! By the way, Arthur called me."

My stomach twisted. "I am so sorry. I can't believe I messed up his name. How mad is he?"

My manager lightly laughed. "Well, he didn't seem mad. He

just told me what happened. Hey, don't let it eat at you." He walked away.

"Sure." My insides were churning.

All I knew was that I did not want to run into the CEO anytime soon. He was the CEO, and I messed up his FIRST name. Who does that?

A week or so later I was walking through the atrium during the busy lunchtime, and I saw him. It was the CEO. We were going to cross paths if I did not take evasive measures. There were people everywhere. All I needed to do was casually move to the right and I would be out of his path. I certainly did not want to be chastised by the CEO in such a public setting. I made my move and veered off to the right as I picked up my pace.

I looked up and there he was right in front of me. Before I could react, he smiled.

"Hi, I heard the class for the new store managers went very well. Congratulations."

"Thank you."

He smiled and walked on. My stomach went from knots to butterflies. From that day forward, whenever he saw me in the hallway, in meetings, no matter where we were, he always acknowledged me.

This CEO had character traits including forgiveness, sensitivity, and compassion. He understood people and he cared about them, no matter what level they held in the organization.

Leaders' behaviors are a clear reflection of their true character. It does not matter what they say about themselves or what they try and make you believe.

In the first example, the leader's behavior clearly identified his self-serving and dehumanizing character. In the case with the CEO, he clearly showed his understanding of the pain I was feeling and went out of his way to let me know, all was OK. I had been on this job for three weeks. He was not my direct manager, yet he left a lasting impression. He set the standard for my expectations for all CEOs.

We all have character traits we want to believe we have and those we want others to think we possess. Behaviors and decisions are reflections of our true character.

The challenge is this: Is the leader aware of his or her behaviors and how it colors their character in the eyes of those around them? It may be precisely how they want to be seen, or it might be something entirely different.

CONSIDER:

• **As a leader to new followers, you may be one of the most influential leaders they will ever have.** New followers are sponges and looking to learn and grow. You could be the one they tell positive stories about 20 or even 30 years later. It is an incredible opportunity to help those new to the work environment build confidence and belief in themselves. It is a privilege and a responsibility as a leader.

• **Having the X-Factor—The Three Cs of Communication, Charisma, and Character**—might determine if when you look over your shoulder you see followers behind you, or a big empty parking lot. Followers are required to be leaders.

• **For those arrogant colleagues, it may very well be that they are frustrated or frightened.** The colleague who joined our team from the field must have been going through an incredibly difficult transition. Introduced as a star, knowing little about the mechanics of the new job, not wanting to ask out of fear as being unqualified, yet sinking. It must have been a terrible time for him. He suffered alone. Do yourself a favor, ask for help. People love to help.

CHAPTER THREE

NO ONE COULD HAVE PREDICTED THIS

THE Y2K EXPERIENCE

If you have been around long enough, you might remember Y2K. The phenomena that was in every headline throughout the entire year of 1999. If you were not around, you might get a great laugh from this story. For those asking, "What is Y2K?," well, Y2K was the nickname for the Year 2000 software bug. It represented a computer coding problem that was going to wreak havoc on anything that used computerized systems on January 1, 2000, which, even in the year 2000, was virtually everything. For those of us that recall living through this event, we were warned about a mini-Armageddon coming midnight, December 31, 1999.

The cover of *Time* magazine in January 1999, spoke to the sheer insanity of the Y2K world. In all seriousness, we were on the edge of our seats for a good twelve months as we lived each day up to December 31, 1999.

The problem, in a nutshell, was this: Computer programs were written to abbreviate the full year to two digits. Instead of "1998," they would store "98" to save memory space. When the programs were written, they did not anticipate the turn of the century to 2000. So, the challenge was that those programs were going to possibly read "00" as "1900," or be unable to recognize it at all. When the clock struck January 1, 2000, there was fear that computers would not be able to operate correctly.

Y2K brought fear of electrical grids going down. No one would have electricity. Planes wouldn't be able to land because traffic control systems were going to collapse. Water would become contaminated as water purification plants would stop functioning. We were instructed to load up on bottled water and enough non-perishable food for a month in anticipation of a global meltdown. The advice of panicked experts was to keep a copy of your last bank statements, so you knew how much money you had in the bank in the event the entire banking networks were wiped out.

The clock struck midnight.

Nothing.

The lights stayed on and water sources did not become contaminated. Planes landed. The fireworks went off around the globe as they had every year prior.

To prevent the potential meltdown of society as we knew it, companies shifted all available resources to their IT teams who worked overtime for months to correct the date programming problem. All resources were put in place to protect the company's assets and ensure that business activities could continue into the new year.

As a world, we were prepared to be immobilized in ways we had never imagined. Y2K ended up being a non-event for the most part. It became the spotlight on the incredible dependency the world had come to have on technology.

It was a huge leadership challenge. IT teams required mobilization to correct coding and also keep the business functioning. The entire employee population needed to remain focused on their responsibilities as the fear of a global meltdown loomed.

PERSONAL IMPACT OF CHANGE

During the 1990s, technology was often discussed regarding the impact it would have on the workplace. How work was completed would continue to change with new technological advances. Available information would continue to grow exponentially. Within the work environment, the benefits and the strains of the rapid advancement of information explosion was recognized. Philosophical discussions about the impact occurred around conference room tables, during strategic planning sessions, and over lunches.

In all those discussions, no one could have predicted how the advancement of technology would impact personal lives and ultimately how that impact would carry into the workplace.

The question was asked, "What is the greatest challenge leaders face today?" By far, the number one response was change. Not just any change. The rapid pace of change, the sheer number of changes, and the unprecedented advancement of technology disrupting business and altering our daily lives.

The Y2K experience gripped the world. The difference was everyone was focused on the same technology challenge. That seems like nothing compared to the technology changes faced today and anticipated in our future. The changes and accompanying challenges come from every direction. Now we must decide which challenge we will take on. Which matters to us and our business? What is the priority for resource availability?

TECHNOLOGY CHANGE HAS OUTPACED HUMAN BIOLOGY

The floating-point operations per second (FLOPS) is a metric for computer performance. It measures the speed of a computer in operations per second. There has been a trillion-fold increase in FLOPS since the 1950s and by all indications, it is going to get faster as technology advances continue. The processing power of the brain? Not much change since the 1950s. However, because of technology advances, each day, humans are hit with more data and information, more distractions than ever before.

Twenty years ago, communication classes taught that all the information received in one day was equivalent to what people were exposed to over a lifetime just 50 years prior. Who knows what that looks like today? There are billions of websites, millions of apps, thousands of TV stations, podcasts, and radio stations. All these information channels share stories, news, truth, and misinformation. What information can be trusted? That is one of the most significant questions we face today.

Add in every social media platform, texting, messenger, chat apps, and the old-fashioned phone call. It's no wonder why people are so distracted. Employees were reprimanded for playing solitaire on their desktop in the past. They do not need their workstation for everything that distracts them any longer. They have their smartphones. Now they compare notes on the games they play at work. It is acceptable. "I am stuck on level 189. Does anyone know the trick to getting past this level?" This is no longer an uncommon question during work hours. Yes, things have changed. What is acceptable has changed.

Until 1980, television stations used to go off the air around midnight or shortly after that. From midnight until early morning, television screens were nothing but "snow" and the sound of static. In the morning, the color bar test pattern would come on the screen in preparation for the days broadcasting. Then came the first 24-hour station. ESPN launched in 1979, and if sports wasn't your thing, CNN brought 24-hour news to viewers in 1980. We used to be forced to do something besides watch television. Now, almost all channels broadcast around the clock.

Our challenge today is not obtaining information. The challenge today is sifting through the data to find the trusted and the truthful. There is an overflow of input with the available technology, social media, and the constant bombardment of information. There are pinging notifications from your favorite sites, apps, health monitoring, groups, e-mails, calendars, texting, and the list goes on. If your devices are not pinging, those sitting next to you are pinging. And there are those that have no problem texting and having the "boink" sound of each letter typed sound off to everyone around them. We live in a state of potential distractions.

How does a leader maintain focus and engagement of employees if those employees are constantly distracted? The blessing of information at our fingertips becomes the Trojan horse. The accelerated pace of so many changes was not within our vocabulary a short time ago. Everyone has had to learn how to adjust, including the leaders.

An executive once said, "Leave your personal life at the door. This building is a place of business." Can you imagine the pile of smartphones sitting at the front door of all the buildings? Seriously, can you believe the mutiny if everyone was told to leave his or her smartphones at home? We are now connected to our personal and professional lives daily, 24/7. The daily path of personal and professional connections is intertwined, and there is little chance of separating them ever again.

Companies are now learning how to use personal smartphones to their advantage. Need to track expenses? There is an app for that. Put that on your phone, please. Need to get a message out quickly? Use texting or apps for specific groups. Require documents signed? There is an app for that also. Just load them on your phone, please.

I remember seeing an episode of an old favorite show with two famous crime fighters. Robin asked Batman why he carried a fish in his belt. Batman replied that all crime fighters carry what they need in their utility belts.

The smartphone is our utility belt—the device full of tools, as well as distractions. Not one person could have predicted this 20 years ago when the discussion revolved around the information explosion in business.

Leaders face this challenge with their employees every day. Engagement requires being present. Being present requires focus and the ability to mitigate distractions. Yet technology is required to be competitive. To be successful. To make money.

In one company, there was an entire stream of discussion surrounding a popular game involving exploding candy. There was admiration for the game's ability to focus the player's attention and continually to draw the player into the game. There was acknowledgement of the brilliance of game creators and how well they understood brain mechanics. There were discussions to understand how performance processes might be gamified to increase the level of employee engagement. If only there was a way to engage employees at the same level games engaged players?

Therein lies the challenge for leaders. How to use technology productively to better the organization while minimizing employees' time spent on non-productive activities on a device that they carry with them daily and completely flip out if the battery runs out or they lose it. Engagement is a continual challenge and advancing technology will not reduce the available distractions.

THE PACE OF CHANGE

The exponential speed of change, along with the continually increasing number of changes, causes companies always to be asking, "What's next?" The element of time is now, more than ever, a critical competitive necessity. The pressure is on for companies to constantly respond to new competitive services, products, and industry disrupters.

Amazon is an industry disruptor with its vast product selection, pricing, and shipping. It has changed the way we shop and has changed the level of service expected from all online retailers. Companies in the line of fire from the disruptors don't have much time to react to changes. Customers are quick to ask, "Why not you? Why can't I receive the same service from you?"

Strategic change in a company is no longer an occasionally occurring event. Change is now the standard. It may not always be an overarching strategic change, but each change can impact strategy and operations. A fast transition is good for business. Rapid transition is not good for people. The price has been the reduction of trust and confidence of the employees in their companies and their leaders. See if any of these sound familiar?

"Are you kidding? We just changed the system."

"Why are we changing again?"

"Does anyone know what they're doing around here?"

Yes, they do know what they are doing. However, another response to the competition making a strategic move is required. Change in laws requires immediate responses. Another innovation is realized that now disrupts business systems. Another improvement or enhancement is determined a necessity. It is change, after change, after change. There are so many changes! Employees question the capability of the company's leadership. This constant change begins to chip away at the employees' trust in the organization. Employees struggle to keep up. Change fatigue is a real problem.

The daily erosion of confidence and belief in leadership is a constant challenge. The layers of stress for all employees, including the leaders, begins to take a toll. If any one of the changes has even a hint of violating a stated company value, the erosion of trust propagates.

Research also shows that many employees do not trust communications from leadership. Employees believe they are only getting a part of the story, a portion of the truth, and may believe that the communications are full of lies.

Change is not easy. The exponential speed of change results in humans adapting to the change they face at different paces depending on their capacity and willingness to change. Leaders must adapt and communicate differently to reflect what is happening in the current environment. But do they know how?

Everyone is looking for the next stressor to happen. It is like the Y2K event, sitting on the edge of your seat, waiting for something to happen. Unless you are a change junkie—and some folks are—it is hard. Sometimes it is even difficult for a change lover. No one is exempt from the impact of change.

SPRINT, EAT, SLEEP, REPEAT

Our ancestors had bodies and minds that spent many years with a lifestyle that looked like this:

Sprint. Hunt. Eat. Rest.

Sprint. Hunt. Eat. Rest.

Sprint. Hunt. Eat. Rest.

Moreover, even when life became a bit busier during the day, life was still slower in the evenings and on the weekends. Those living in the winter climates had incredibly slow lives during the cold months. We rested more. We relaxed a lot more.

Today lifestyle looks a lot like this:

Wake Up. Check messages/emails/social media.

Sprint. Drive. Drive through. Sprint. Drop the kids off.

Check messages/emails/social media.

Sprint. Work. Lunch. Sprint.

Check messages/emails/social media.

Work.

Check messages/emails/social media.

Pick the kids up. Sprint. Drive.

Check messages/emails/social media.

Activities.

Sprint.

Check messages/emails/social media.

With or without children, there is always something filling time. Errands. Volunteer work. Commitments. Pets. Family. Our weekends, which used to be a time of slowing down and collecting ourselves, are now full of sprinting and completing the next task, the next errand, the next project. We are now often always on the move. There is no end. If we are not moving, we have our smart devices nearby to stay connected. If it is not work-related, it is family, friends, side gigs, games, or social media taking our attention. We are overwhelmed with all the things we feel we must do.

WHO IS MAKING DINNER?

Fifteen years ago, a corporate headquarters with a large cafeteria decided to support its employees who were feeling overwhelmed by providing take-home meals for purchase. The chatter around the cooler sounded like this:

"Who would do that?"

"What? They can't even cook their dinner?"

It was shortly thereafter that no one heard much more about those take-home meals. What was interesting was watching a company look for ways to support their busy employees and the backlash heard around the water cooler. Today, employees look to their companies to help them ease the burden of every day challenges. Employees look for services to make their life easier.

Today there are food services that deliver boxes of prepackaged gourmet meals. No one questions it anymore. Food delivery from grocery stores is now an excellent solution for many households. Now, users of food services share their experiences so other families can find the best solutions.

Walk into any grocery store, and there are packages of food ready to take home and cook up for dinner. Grab a bag with everything included! Heat it and eat it! Deals on ready-to-eat meals are always available. Many grocery stores now offer areas to sit and eat, drink a beer, have a glass of wine, or enjoy some sushi.

If you visit these grocery stores on the weekend, these socializing areas are busy. Need an exciting place for a first date? How about the wine and cheese counter at the grocery store? It is a cool place to hang out these days. It is a far cry from the wooden floor grocery stores that used to populate the local neighborhoods.

Daily lives are changing. Employees' needs have evolved from a job and a paycheck to asking for help to relax, unwind and re-energize. Employees look to their employers to help them. There are examples of companies supporting their employees in every way possible. Shutterstock, housed in the Empire State Building, provides a rooftop terrace for spectacular views of the city for relaxation and outdoor meetings. L.L. Bean offers pop-up outdoor workspaces. Microsoft provides treehouses fully equipped with Wi-Fi, power, and a relaxing atmosphere. Amazon offers treehouse meeting rooms and open spaces surrounded by plants and waterfalls. Kasper offers nap pods and shaded terrace outdoor workstations. Companies are working hard, and with great creativity, to provide areas other than traditional workspaces to support employees in their desire to be productive in more engaging surroundings. Companies are finding ways to provide engagement with employees outside skill growth and personal development.

Employees are looking for ways to destress, relax, and get away from the cubicle. Companies are responding. The number of hours worked continues to be high. The commute time has increased for many. Employees have many options these days. The dollar amount on the paycheck is no longer the sole focus. Companies are continually negotiating ways to help employees focus, engage, and delight them with the goal of improved engagement and increased discretionary effort.

Leaders have now been tasked with not only leading the business, but also leading the development of solutions to assist employees solve their daily challenges. That expectation was not on the table a few years ago. Leaders were focused on business and not employee issues, unless it impacted business. The role of the leader now includes how to create an environment that draws employees to the company, maintain engagement (and that has many facets), and assists the employee population in finding new ways to be productive that includes their mental health and physical comfort.

This requires the leader to be in tune with employees of all generations, needs, and differing work styles. Providing differentiation in employee support services is now a competitive advantage.

COMPETITIVE ENVIRONMENTS
CALL FOR QUICK RESPONSES

The need to quickly respond to the competitive environment often requires leaders to get together at a moment's notice and make big decisions. Even with short notice, they could take weeks or even months to develop the next strategic move, discuss the options, develop a plan, and identify resources. Now that this one problem is solved, companywide communications go out to the masses, and leaders direct their sights to the next hill and start climbing.

Managers are now in the role of executing the plan with their employees. Meanwhile, managers and employees are adjusting to the recent announcement. Leaders are full of expectations that the organization will deliver on the plan and quickly. Delay causes frustration. Leaders wonder why the plan is not getting executed. The employees are wondering what to do and what is next. Managers are squeezed in the middle as they are expected to deliver and manage the process of change with their employees. Managers rarely get the support they need to navigate all the elements of change much less their own internal reactions to change. Yet, most organizations do not provide managers the tools to execute the change nor support their employees through the change process.

LEADERS NEED FOLLOWERS

The rapid pace of change leaves leaders looking behind them to see a smattering of followers. The employee population often takes a wait-and-see approach wondering if this next change will stick or go by the wayside. After all, two-thirds of all strategic plans fail, and some say that number is rising. It's a constant push-pull, tug-of-war, will-they-or-won't-they situation with any change process. There is even a name for failed strategic plans: Strategic Plans on the Shelf (SPOTS). Strategic plan documents are saved because one day they will go back and do it again, but not make the same mistakes they made before. They are binders that collect dust.

Change models suggest that with any change, 10 percent of the population affected are going to be early adopters. You know, those camping outside certain stores in the snow, rain or blazing sun, all in a quest to purchase that latest smart gadget.

There is also the 10 percent on the other side of the curve—those who will not adapt to the change, period. In this 10 percent would be the gentleman I met at a coffee shop recently. He was reading a book. I sat down in the chair across from him. He stopped long enough to look up and make a comment about my smartphone, factually stating he would never purchase one of those things—not a flip phone, not a cell phone. Nada. Wires connected his only phone to his wall.

The remaining 80 percent of the employees sit in the middle, waiting. Waiting to see which way the wind blows this time. Some will gravitate towards the change out of obligation, but not fully step over the line. Some will be curious and watch to see what others are doing in response to the news. Others will want to wait and see of the change takes hold before disrupting their current work processes. Why change the way they do things if it is only going to go back to the way it was? It is that 80 percent—those pausing, waiting, and hesitating—that leaders must focus on with unrelenting attention and clarity in messaging. The sheer number of changes impacting organizations are significantly increasing these days. Leaders' attention on the communication processes, with more frequent and detailed explanations for that 80 percent, has the ability to drive engagement and ease stress. Too often, the failure to provide the necessary additional communications and create manager support mechanisms is sidestepped as the leaders charge the next hill. Leaders get agitated. They just want the plan executed, they want it done. Employees scramble to make things happen.

Managers get caught in the middle as they deal with the employees' struggle with change, as well as their personal reactions to the announcements. It is no wonder change efforts fail.

The speed of change is impacting every person, every process, and every decision. Leaders struggle to create an environment where they can glance over their shoulder and see most of their employees joyfully following close behind. Leaders need followers.

The fact remains that many employees will not speak up to express their concerns, stress, or discomfort. They will hold back. They may fear being labeled as weak, or perhaps not a team player. They may not believe in where the company is going. Or worse yet, they may fear retaliation because of their inability to jump on the next change train. Change fatigue is the new normal for many employees.

Without deliberate attention to the actions after the planning phase, today's environment offers less time for curation of the new. The only way to get through the change process is to pick and choose where efforts will be placed and what will be left on the wayside. Without strong planning and consistent follow-up by all leaders, change effort outcomes will be mediocre at best.

Trust is on the chopping block unless leaders focus on cultivating the right messages quickly and more frequently, rather than later. In these times of extreme change, leaders must engage their followers with more information then they may believe is necessary. Leaders are the constant inspiring drivers of change. Change takes its toll on the leaders as well. They also experience change fatigue.

Whatever you do as a leader, toe the line and don't challenge the boundaries of corporate values. That will create an underlying cause for more distrust and anger. Always bear in mind that with the accelerated pace of change in the workplace, there is a parallel system of change happening in personal lives. There's no end in sight. Employees are human, and they require time to catch up and catch their breath. However, these days, the time never seems to be found.

Leaders must be present with their organization. All levels. Seeing strategic change process through the lens of an executive's meeting room is not effective. Expecting that employees will fall in line behind the initiative can no longer be accepted if actual change is to permeate all areas of the organization.

CONSIDER:

• **Life is now a "round the clock" affair.** We have access to the world around the clock. The world has access to us. Distractions are a reliable constant and the methods used by leaders to engage employees matter. Clear and timely communication is imperative. Supporting managers with tools and coaching on change is a critical business need.

• **New leaders have little or no experience with change.** New leaders have no idea how to deal with change, much less rapid-fire change. They need guidance and coaching on the basics. Coaching is often from leaders who themselves aren't so great at change. They need coaches who have successfully navigated change.

• **Employees spend much of their waking hours at work and are often working at home in the evenings and on the weekends.** They look to the company to help with solutions to reduce stress, cope with the constant change and make their lives more enjoyable. It does not have to be treehouse meeting rooms with waterfalls and flowers. However, to err on the generous side of employee support might create a whole new level of engagement and keep their mindset present while they are at work.

• **Managers need additional support.** They cannot be expected to drive change when they are not provided specific tools to help them engage employees. Managers can no longer be expected to the "tellers" of the answers of change. They need to be the facilitators of engaging conversations to support the transition of their teams. They need tools. They need training.

• **Leaders need followers.** People don't follow just because of a title. There must be more behind the curtain. Leaders must be visible through communication processes at all levels, regularly.

CHAPTER FOUR

THE ONE CHARACTERISTIC

CAN I HAVE TWO?

"What is one characteristic you believe every leader should possess?" I asked. "It's tough to pick one. Can I have two?" most responded. I laughed. "Well, let's start with your top one."

Inevitably, those interviewed shared more than one desired leadership characteristic. One individual had a very long list that easily filled up an entire sheet of paper. We focused on the top five. To no surprise, the characteristics they shared as their top choices, directly reflected the leaders they most admired.

What was the top identified characteristic that all leaders should have through the lens of these HR leaders?

Humility.

The top five characteristics identified during the interviews:

• Humility (being humble).

• Decision-Making.

• The Strength to Say No.

• Communication.

• Trust.

These five characteristics were evident throughout the interviews. They were identified in some respect in every story shared.

HUMILITY

Humility, or being humble, was identified as the number one characteristic more times than any other. If not chosen as the top characteristic during an interview, it came in as a close number two.

What does humility mean? From the stories, it spoke to leaders who knew they had important responsibilities. They also knew they could not do it alone. They respectfully asked others to bring their knowledge, experience and passion to the team. They spent little time promoting themselves. Rather, they used air time to communicate the successes and the hard work necessary to achieve those successes.

Humility is a noun and defined as freedom from pride or arrogance. It is the quality or state of being humble. Synonyms for humility include modest and down-to-earth.

Humility is also defined as the quality or state of not thinking you are better than other people. Leaders with humility see themselves as equal to all humans. They define their job as one that requires followers to be successful. They do not allow the title to define them. Instead, they define leadership by their ability to recognize the talent and capabilities of those around them. Leaders hold more power and influence when they are humble.

Humility also has a dark side. Shy, bashful, meek, submissive. Who wants that label? Perhaps the leader's interpretation of humility is dependent on whether he or she is genuinely humble or not?

A leader with humility asks how he/she can grow. Humble leaders possess a constant desire to learn and be better as leaders. New information is a considered a gift. Being wrong? Well, it's okay. It's all about learning and growth.

There are three things expected of leaders:

1. **Do your job**. Requires competence and openness to learning. Admission of not knowing all the answers requires humility.

2. **Hire better than yourself**. It requires humility.

3. **Provide others what they need**. Be a leader who focuses on service. It requires humility and belief in others.

The essence of humility as a leader transcends the formal hierarchy in the organization. You are human. I am human. We are all human. The leader may have more experience, or not. They may have more expertise or not. Suffice it to say the leaders' title may show hierarchy on an organization chart. But as humans, we are equal.

Humility made it to the top of the characteristic list for a reason. We may think differently, act differently, and believe differently, but we are all made from the same stuff. We are made from the same basic atoms that connect and build us as humans.

Having a title as a leader is solely that. A human being with title. Expectations are attached to the title. There is a different level of responsibility with the title.

"Leaders with humility," shared one HR leader, "understand that every time a leader makes a decision, it impacts someone's life and sometimes that impact is significant." A human resource is a human first and a resource second.

Leadership requires awareness of the impact of their actions, behaviors, and decisions. It is not just a business decision. The decision may be best for the business. But what is the impact on the people? Leaders hold power over the lives of others.

Humility, being the number one characteristic, deserves its own chapter, don't you think? Well, not really. Humility is intertwined with so many other qualities.

Being gracious shows humility. Not getting angry when your order is wrong at the restaurant. Showing forgiveness for the error. Genuinely recognizing others, not just reading off names at a meeting to say thanks. Truly appreciating others for their contributions, not believing that folks are just doing their jobs. Asking for ideas on how to accomplish goals, trusting that there are other ways besides "my way." Behaving as though leading others is a privilege and always treating people respectfully. Allowing others to have the floor and take charge, not micro-managing them. Admitting mistakes and accepting responsibility, not blaming others. Being grateful just because. Listening to others with real interest, not wishing they would get to the point so you can get to your business. It is holding the door open for others instead of expecting them to hold the door open for you. It is standing aside in the shadow of the podium and giving the spotlight to others.

Humility is not one thing. Humility is not a skill set. It is a way of being. It is asking yourself how the other person will feel. Humility is hard to teach in a classroom. Being willing to understand and appreciate the impact of actions on others is one good first step to humility.

DECISION MAKING IS A STRONG NUMBER TWO

Making the best decision for the company is not always the best decision for the employee(s). It is one of the reasons why being a leader can be very hard. It is a constant balancing act.

"It is important always to be fair," said one long-time HR executive, "and stick with the core values of the organization, even when the organization is putting pressure to make a decision that would deviate from those values."

Sticking with the core values is not always the easiest action to take. Respecting the company's values and acting accordingly can cost the company money. After all, expenses are to be avoided, not incurred. There is often pressure on leaders to turn a blind eye.

"I'll watch more closely. I won't let it happen again," says the manager. HR often is asked to "let this one go." However, once there is a value violation, it becomes harder over time to hold others accountable for honoring the corporate values. Inequity and favoritism begin to shift the culture to the haves and have-nots.

If one person is held accountable to the values standards, and another one is not, employees begin to talk. The stories and legends of the company take hold. The entire culture begins to suffer. On which side of the line are you standing? Are you a "have?" Are you in the group that get to push the ethics and values lines around a bit? Are you on the side of the line that does not have to follow all the rules? Do all the policies not apply to you? Are you an exception?

Or are you one of the "have-nots?" Are you on the other side of the line that does not allow any rules to be bent? Are you on the side of the line where employees are written up for infractions? The side where exceptions are not made?

If all employees are not held accountable to following the written and agreed upon statements overarching the company, then nothing matters. Inequity, often hoped to be hidden from the have-nots, rarely remains hidden. Privilege is now the new lens for those that can do as they wish with little consequence, or no consequence. Bitterness becomes a part of the vocabulary for employees.

All is great for those on the "have" side of the line, until something happens, and they are now placed on the "have-not" side. The sense of violation and feeling of disrespect is enormous and they are quick to share their sense of violation. It is not always easy to resolve their frustration.

Leaders make decisions every day. Equity and fairness are not the same. Values and policies are not the same. Individual circumstances must be evaluated every day. Often leaders may make decisions that are confidential in support of individual circumstances. Those circumstances must remain confidential. Leaders want to support employees through their journey and changing needs even though other employees may feel slighted.

Policies may state that all employees must be at work at 8:00 a.m. A value of the organization is that all employees are important to the growth and success of the organization. Allowing employees to arrive at 10:00 a.m. because they have medical treatment or a temporary family need may not follow policy, but fully supports the value of the organization. Terminating an employee for having to arrive at work at 10:00 a.m. is supporting the policy but may not be viewed as living the company values.

Each decision results in a different reaction from the employees in the organization. Employees will decide if they or others have been treated fairly. It is a constant balancing act. If you have been in a leadership role, you will understand this repeating dilemma. Making decisions that support the company's values and ethics statements will drive a culture of fairness, not equity. It is much easier to look at oneself in the mirror each morning with a values-based approach to decisions. Employees are more accepting of deviations from policy if they believe the values of the company are lived daily.

Leaders also have other decision-making challenges. Leaders may only view a situation based on data and facts immediately in their field of view. They may only see their immediate pain point. They may make decisions that result in outcomes that are solely for their own benefit.

Decisions that are self-serving over the company good is an unfortunate carrot dangling in front of some leaders. Making numbers, so that big bonuses are paid out, is too much of an opportunity for some leaders to pass up. Decisions to reach short-term goal numbers at whatever cost is painful for the organization and will often result in an adverse rippling effect to all parts of the company. It can take months if not years to recover, all for the bank account or longevity of the executive. It happens.

There are many fiduciary pressures that impact leaders' decisions. There are pressures from executives and shareholders for certain outcomes. Sometimes those pressures may cause decisions that may not reflect the company's value statements. It is a constant balancing act. Sometimes it is a balancing act between doing the right thing, or not.

As one HR leader shared, "Leaders don't get paid big bucks because they are special. They get paid the big bucks because leadership is often a lonely and crappy job. They must make decisions that no one else would want to have to make."

IT'S ONLY TWO BUCKS

For one leader, after months of high turnover, inability to fill jobs, and compensation market studies ignored for one plant location, her frustration came to a head during a senior staff meeting. She was at her wit's end.

The senior leaders of the organization were constantly repeating their guiding principle statement, "We are market competitive in our pay and benefits." However, the direction to undercut pay and benefits of the market was the unstated and expected mode of operation. This state of operating was driven by one executive. Everyone else fell in line.

The facility was having a tough time hiring, and it had been going on for over a year. The recruiter could not get jobs filled. Production goals were a daily joke because they could never be met. That meant financial goals could never be met. There were not enough people to run the facility. Those that remained were demoralized and angry. They were overworked and felt taken advantage of because open jobs were never filled. The employees were tired. Employees believed that not filling open positions was an intentional cost savings plan by senior leadership. The local HR team was exasperated. However, that did not stop the constant pressure on the facility to make their numbers.

The HR leader built a business case to get the situation headed in the right direction. She targeted the staff meeting to discuss the problem. She looked for support from her peers to help negotiate a better solution. She was prepared to take on the executive and push for a reasonable solution. She knew it was going to be a difficult discussion as the culture for this organization was one of "That's what the boss wants, so we have to do it."

The fear of this one executive had minimized the effectiveness of the entire senior leadership team over time. This determined HR leader was newer and not willing to live in that camp. She was ready to stand alone in her quest to do the right thing for this facility.

She came to the table armed with all the data including facility numbers, market research, interview feedback, and exit interview results. She made the recommendation to pay the market rate of $20 per hour. She shared all the information she had. The facility was failing. The downward spiral was getting worse by the day. The good employees were leaving at an alarming rate. If the facility was fully staffed, the remaining employees' skills would be upgraded with training. Ideally, many would be replaced. At this point, neither training nor replacement was an option. The entire facility was teetering on the cliff of complete failure.

"Eighteen dollars an hour. That is what we will pay. I don't care if the studies say the going rate is $20. It's close enough. It is only a $2 difference. It amounts to 80 bucks a week. Who will miss that? It saves us money as it adds up annually per person," was the response of the executive.

No amount of conversation was going to shift this executive's decision. He thought himself quite clever. And not one person around the table pushed back, except for the determined HR leader. Not one person around the table wanted to support the right decision out of fear for the wrath of the executive.

After the meeting, the hallway conversations were vibrant with frustration. Those who did not speak up at the meeting were now full of bravado in comments and professing their frustration for not making the right decision. But not at the meeting table.

A good business decision? Thinking of the bottom line? Saving that valuable financial resource? Let's examine this decision as seen through the determined leader's viewpoint.

As you can imagine, like most companies, there were values and governance statements about treating employees respectfully and acting fairly. And don't forget the articulation of "competitive wages and benefits."

Anyone who is making around $40,000 a year is probably not living a life of expensive cars and designer shoes. They are most likely managing every dime and if they have a family, it becomes even more closely managed. If there is an opportunity to make over $4,000 a year more by leaving the job that pays $18 an hour, versus one that pays $20 an hour, most likely they are gone.

If someone is making around $40,000 a year, he or she does probably does not have a robust savings account. They need that extra money. That two dollars, which sounds like such a trivial amount in the boardroom, has a tremendous impact on a family surviving on that salary. Those 80 bucks per week can be the difference between food on the table or none.

From a business process standpoint, recruiting and acquiring talent is not free, nor is it cheap. Not paying to the market in a competitive talent landscape results in frustrating efforts to find employees. Training new employees and ramping them up to acceptable productivity costs the organization financially. The intense pressure on current employees to work extra hours to meet deadlines and make up the work for those vacant positions, results in burnt out employees who become bitter and angry. Employees in that situation have reduced engagement and productivity and, occasionally, their behavior gets a little dicey. These employees will take more time off. They are not bad people; they are exhausted and stretched too far. It is evident that the decision of paying two dollars an hour less than the market demanded was not such a good idea, except in the eyes of the one executive, the one who held the cards.

Crazy story? Yes.

True story? Yes.

This story is an example of poor decision-making and frankly, lack of leadership humility. The arrogance of the leader's desire to be the cleverest in the room only hurt the organization. The cost of arrogance does not show up on in a line item in the spreadsheet. In this example, the impact was much costlier than that two dollars per hour.

Dismissing the values. Ignoring the data. Ego driven. It's destructive at best.

THE ANSWER IS STILL NO

Employee's watch for alignment between company values, strategies, and leadership decisions. They carefully monitor known corporate values and leadership behavior. They watch closely. The inability to say no, or the inability to state the same message in front of the door as well as behind the door, strains the organization.

Employees listen to what leaders say. They listen to word choices. They observe whether values are honored in decisions. If there is any lack of alignment, any perceived deviation from the company values, trust in leadership erodes. Leaders staying in integrity with their words and actions will not generate much reaction. It is expected. Falling out of integrity can have devastating results.

Staying in integrity as a leader does not always come easy. It does, however, make the difference between looking over one's shoulder and seeing their team ready to charge the next hill, or seeing no one and hearing crickets.

Have you ever had a time when an edict came down from a senior executive to stop all current work and shift to a last-minute project? You could not see the higher value of this one project over the ones currently in progress. However, it was clear that the leader had made a promise to someone, and he was going to make it happen. He was going to keep his word. This meant the entire team's work was going to have to shift.

What did you do?

Did you follow the edict?

Did you say no?

How did you respond?

Sometimes a leader needs to say no. They need to say no if they are to successfully deliver on projects and meet goals. Those goals are agreed upon during collective operational planning, meaning all the leaders agree these projects are important strategically. For a leader to say no, may require them to dig deep and find their brave heart. Under intense pressure, many leaders give in and say yes. The belief that being a team player requires saying yes, is strong. That belief is often misguided.

The information technology (IT) team always seem to receive requests to "slip this one project in, please." And if they say no, the senior leader who benefits from this project might use their "title muscle." They might say, "Go tell them to slide this in. If you have a problem, let me know." Oh, those words, "Let me know." They drive irritation, erode relationships, yet ultimately, the "slide in project" gets done.

"If you have a problem, let me know." No one likes that. However, it causes action and reaction.

EXCEPT FOR THIS ONE TIME

During a weekly leadership meeting for a large company, Tony (not his real name) was instructed by his manager, a senior executive, to put all current projects aside for a last-minute project.

An agreement had been made between this top executive and a very persuasive department leader that an IT project would get done. The decision was made without discussing it with Tony or any other executive peers. The executive was feeling like he was going to be the hero for this department leader. There was an expectation that Tony would comply.

Tony and his team were executing significant IT projects for the organization, projects which supported corporate strategic plans. The projects impacted the entire global employee base.

When Tony was instructed to prioritize this one project, Tony said, "No." He continued, "We cannot make any shifts in our projects at this time. All IT resources are executing strategic plans agreed upon by the executives of the company. My team will not deviate as the impact is too disruptive."

The executive was visibly irritated. The HR leader leaned forward over the table and said, "You must do what your manager tells you to do. If you do not, you are insubordinate."

Tony turned to the HR leader and replied, "We will not deliver on our current strategic projects if we prioritize this one project. I also know we cannot deliver your requested project in the time frame requested. The answer is no. This deviation results in nothing but failure. I refuse to set my team up for failure. The answer is no." Tony's team member, who was sitting in the room watching this exchange play out, was frozen. "Tony is going to get himself in trouble," was the only thought that raced through his mind.

Tony always told his team, "I will not set any of us up for failure." At that very moment, the realization was that what Tony said in front of the door, was precisely what he said behind the door. His actions and words aligned even under extreme pressure to change course. He was living in a state of integrity.

Tony was considering more than just his team. He had made commitments to the entire executive team. He committed his team to contribute to the strategic success of the company. He promised delivery of a working, error-free solution, and on time. His team focused on those three elements. Tony stayed in integrity to the entire organization. There would be no apologies. There would be no erosion of relationships. There would be no diversion from key timelines agreed upon by the organization on vital operational goals. He lived his words. He was not about to deviate to fulfill one promise made by one executive, who made a decision in a vacuum, at the expense of the organization or his team.

News spread quickly. A team that already admired Tony as a leader was energized more than ever before. When Tony looked over his shoulder, they were all tapping their feet ready to take off with him, wherever he needed them to go.

Another leader may have felt the need to shift all the resources to this other project to fulfill the requirements of the one leader, who made one promise, without engaging critical parts of the organization. Another leader may have succumbed to the threat of insubordination. The result would only derail the progress of many other departments, many other projects, and the fulfillment of strategic obligations. As one HR leader stated," The desire to please everybody results in pleasing only a few."

They say there are moments that define a leader. This was one of those moments for Tony. Having a team member observe Tony's response secured the belief in him as a leader. You can bet that one moment escalated the team's effort and their desire to successfully complete any and all projects.

It takes tremendous courage to say no. Sometimes, it may be the best decision.

COMMUNICATE SOME MORE

Without intentional communication, expectations will be misinterpreted. Expectations, if not explicit, will be assumed and that rarely ends up in the right place. If communications are not provided to update and educate employees, they will fill in the blanks with their own stories and interpretations. Welcome to the birth of rumors. Communication was another capability identified as necessary for successful leaders.

BLACK INK VERSUS RED INK

Holidays are a big deal for the retail industry. Retail organizations need every team member supporting holiday plans. It can be the difference between successfully achieving holiday sales goals or realizing mediocre sales, even worse, falling short of sales goals. We all know holidays are meaningful for retail, but many don't understand the work for the holiday push begins long before the holiday months. It's a huge ramp up to prepare all the products, marketing, and employees who work in retail. Those in the industry know that when holidays roll around, it is all-hands-on-deck.

One executive leader engaged her organization for the upcoming holiday season with very intentional communication strategies. It all began with pre-holiday rallies where expectations were shared in detail. Goals were publicly stated. Each department was given airtime to define their commitment to making the holiday plans successful. Each department leader communicated their specific goals and their plans for achieving those goals. Each leader detailed how they supported other departments as well as their expected contribution to the overarching organizational goals. There was no holding back. It was the full Monty. It created public accountability and transparency for everyone to see.

The rallies positively influenced associates who were instrumental in leading the daily customer service experience on the retail floor. They felt supported and a part of the greater team. They were not just sales associates. They were one of the many essential links in building success. All employees clearly understood the work that had been done up to the day of the rally, the work currently in progress, and the work required in the future.

The ability to engage the entire organization by openly sharing brought public visibility to roles and goals, and it set forth future expectations with great clarity. The executive leader knew how to engage the entire population. She knew that the retail sales associates were an integral part of achieving holiday sales goals.

The sales associates felt valued. They could see how departments had fulfilled obligations to get the product to the selling floor and how marketing plans were supporting the products. They understood why last-minute system upgrades were implemented which resulted in them having to learn new computer register processes.

The rallies were intended to show the effort required of everyone for organizational success. All the teams mattered. It was about the collective effort of everyone. It was all success, or there was no success.

Sharing the vision, the roadmap, the expectations, and commitments engages employees. It treats them as they should be, as part of the entire success chain. It improves discretionary effort. It lays the path for future success.

Whether it is communicating holiday plans, strategic direction, or organization goals, it all matters to the employee. Employees want to know what impacts them directly. They want to know how these changes impact their department and the work they perform. Employees follow their leader, not the entire company. Employees want to engage with their immediate manager to more fully understand shared information.

BUT CAN I TRUST YOU?

Trustworthiness. When you read the chapter on "first leaders," there was a reflection about a leader that gave implicit trust in the new employee's capability to succeed. The employee knew that the leader had her back, would always speak highly of her, and truly wanted her to succeed. That level of trust is not often given, especially to a new employee. In turn for the explicit trust in the new employee, the employee reciprocated with implicit trust in the leader.

Trust takes time to build and yet can be destroyed in a split second. The person that breaks trust, sometimes does not even know what they have done. Trust can be tricky like that. What may seem like absolutely nothing to one person, may trigger a massive internal reaction in someone else.

Trust is foundational to great relationships. It is important for business success. It enables us to go through life with a lot less stress. How is that?

Every time you come to an intersection, you trust that the people driving from the other direction are going to stop at the stop sign. When you choose a dish at a restaurant, you trust the food on your plate is just what you ordered. When you pay with cash, you trust that the change will be accurate. There are many areas of our lives that we believe will be as we expect it to be. We trust that people will do they are supposed to do. That relieves our need to worry. However, once trust is broken, it is challenging to regain it. If someone was hit by a car running a red light, every red light and stop sign now causes apprehension and worry. If a cashier messes up giving back change from a cash transaction, the person receiving their change will begin counting their change each time to make sure it is right. Often, we trust that things are going to operate as designed, and people will do as expected. That assumed trust is not always given to leaders.

It does not take a scientist to tell anyone that leaders are not always trusted. Ask any employee. But what creates a lack of trust? It might be the leader, or it might be the employee.

Here is a partial list. I am sure you have other reasons that can be added.

• Leaders are not held accountable for their actions.

- Leaders are held accountable for their actions. However, it is not shared, so there is a belief there is no accountability.
- Leaders react negatively to news or feedback they do not like.
- Leaders react to things that they are perceiving incorrectly.
- Leaders have been caught in lies.
- Leaders are perceived to be caught in lies when they are just caught in the middle of organization stuff.
- Leaders' behaviors are questionable.
- Leaders violate ethics, values, or disregard policies.
- Leaders have obvious favorites.
- Leaders make decisions that negatively impact employees.
- Employees hear rumors about leaders.
- Employees hear myths or legends about an incident with a leader.
- Employees have been previously "burned" by a leader.
- Employees may hold the belief that there are no leaders that can be trusted.
- Lack of communication causes employees to fill in the blanks.

Trust in leadership has a huge impact on culture. In one company, the leadership culture developed around drinking alcohol. Leaders drank liquor throughout the day. Executive assistants were known to swig out of a flask while at their desk. Of course, there was a rule against drinking while at work and any employee knew if they showed up to work drunk on alcohol, they would be terminated immediately. But not the leaders. This selective rule application drove deep mistrust in the organization. The leaders had no intention of stopping, and no intention in letting employees off the hook.

It was well known in another organization that one executive would be "toasted" by lunchtime. How can decisions be trusted when they are made by an executive who is drunk by noon? How can an organization be trusted when an executive is visibly slurring words and incoherent in the work place, and no one seems to care?

In another situation, a leader pulled out cocaine while leaving work one day. He turned to the HR employee walking next to him and said, "You have no idea the stress I am under. This helps me get through the day. It's better than going out into the streets and doing it."

There was no remorse in his voice. No sense of being caught. He merely stated his matter-of-act reasoning for using an illegal drug in the workplace. People knew he was using drugs. They also saw him walk into the building and leave each day with no repercussions. They also saw him repeatedly receive accolades for his accomplishments. The organization accepted his illegal drug use because he was a high producer for the company.

The HR employee knew that reporting him would be a losing battle. She did not want to take on a fight she knew the most senior HR executive had chosen to ignore. She could not trust him not to throw her under the bus.

Stories like these are ones heard by employees at all levels of the organization. Leaders turning a blind eye to behavior by high producing employees. These stories feed mistrust and confirm suspicions that leaders can't be trusted. Leaders must always be looking for these gaps in their organizations. Moreover, they must listen carefully when these gaps come to their attention.

THE FORMULA

One individual uses a trustworthiness formula to understand not only his challenges developing trust with others, but also as a coaching tool to help improve relationships. It is not the trust equation that will be found when doing an online search. No one could tell me where it came from, and my research resulted in no information on the developer. So, I am sharing it here with no accolades for its developer because no one seems to know.

Trust = (Credibility X Relationship) / Risk

Credibility: You may have heard about me but may not have experienced me.

Relationship: What is the strength of the relationship? Is it new? Have we been best buds for a long time? Are we friends socially or professionally?

Risk: If we work together well and we agree on the outcome, the risk is low. If my engagement is going to cost me, the risk is high.

As with any equation, if any number is 0, trust is 0, and therefore trust is not possible. If credibility is high, but our relationship is in its early stages, the numerator will be lower. The higher the denominator, the lower the trust score. You can plug in the numbers to get a sense of the equation. The benefit of this simple equation is that it provides three elements to determine where trust is troubled and what areas can be addressed to improve trust.

This trust equation is a tool that can be used when forming teams, team interventions, coaching for improved relationships and for assisting leaders in awareness of their impact on others. However, it is only a tool. The real work is addressing the gap.

The thing is, leaders can improve their trustworthiness reputation. Simple actions such as making decisions that align with the stated values contributes to the leader's image. Treating employees fairly on a regular basis, which is not the same as treating them equally. Protecting the rights of all employees by upholding laws that impact the workplace. Putting the safety and security of the employees above profits. Being respectful to all employees. These actions can create trusted bonds between leaders and employees. Trusted leaders will have employees who will move mountains for them. But trust is a fragile state. It only takes one misstep to damage a leader's trustworthiness. The leader can repair the trust bond, if they know that trust has been broken. Sometimes they are completely unaware of how their actions have impacted the employees. Whether the leader is aware of the breach or not, employees are always watching and evaluating the trustworthiness of the leader.

THE FIVE CHARACTERISTICS SUMMARY

As discussed at the beginning of this chapter, five characteristics rose to the top. Hands down, humility came in as the characteristic that was most important.

In every conversation where examples of great leadership were shared, more than one characteristic was in play. Poor leadership stories related the lack of these characteristics. These five—humility, decision-making, the strength to say no, communication, and trust—consistently were a part of every conversation. It is not easy to teach these characteristics. It takes coaching, understanding, behavior identification, impact feedback, and reinforcement. It requires recognition of the fear that hold leaders back from making changes. Most of all, it takes willingness, time, and practice.

CONSIDER:

• **The most noted characteristic identified as most important for leaders is humility**. If you ask an adult to share an experience of humility, they will often share a story of humiliation. The term humility does not always generate a favorable view of leadership strength. True humility is when a person accurately sees their strengths and weaknesses and is willing to grow.

• **The ability to make good decisions based on business need is powerful**. Being able to say no with a brave heart. Influence and engage through communication. And last, be aware of the importance of building trust.

• **Always be open to feedback**. Be prepared to grow. Focus on development. Above all, be humble.

• **Trustworthiness is hard to gain and ease to destroy**. Employees are always watching leadership behaviors and evaluating whether they believe in the leaders or not.

CHAPTER FIVE

DON'T BE A LEADER HACK

I LIKE THEIR STYLE

If you want to have a lot more fun as a leader, be yourself. Learn how to be comfortable in your skin.

There is no single best way to be a leader. Pick up any magazine, and you can find stories about amazing leaders and how they have grown their business. You will find stories of how leaders led their people to incredible levels of success and influence. These stories develop business lore and continue to perpetuate the greatness of the leader. These leaders are admired for their intelligence, creativity, and ability to overcome obstacles, and reach unprecedented levels of success. For leaders who have yet to find their style, they may choose to emulate a great leader they admire or, whom others admire.

Unfortunately, one cannot replicate what another leader has experienced and accomplished over a lifetime. However, it happens. Leaders try to take all the great things these other leaders have done and make it their daily own. You will hear leaders' names shared in meetings. Names like Steve, Jeff, John, Phil, and Brenda are spoken in meetings. Stories are shared about their accomplishments, and the words will be said, "We can learn a lot from what he/she did." Many things can be admired, but be very careful about trying to emulate that leader. There are too many factors that as a leader, you cannot possibly recreate, factors such as:

- The right mindset.
- The right learning experiences.
- The right financial break.
- The right market.
- The right product or service.
- The right economy.
- The right players.
- The right team.
- The right connections.
- The right moves at the right time.

Great leaders are great because they are laser focused on their business. They do not drop a past solution on a current situation and try and make it work. They understand their business, their style, and their needs. They know their clients, customers, products, and services.

When assessing current processes, there are common questions asked by many leaders. What is going well? What is challenging? What is getting in the way of success? What resources are needed?

Applying these questions is a great process to understand the landscape and unleash awareness and learning with the team. These are excellent questions no matter what department or function you are leading. However, it's not trying to be someone else. It's using a tool at your disposal to think through your unique situation.

COMFORTABLE IN MY SKIN

Some leaders are not comfortable in their skin. If you have not heard that description before, it means to be clear and confident in your beliefs, your strengths, your abilities, your choices. It is also finding comfort with your gaps, flaws, and imperfections. It is remaining open to learning how to close these gaps.

The richest way to develop an unobstructed view of oneself is by interacting with others and then asking for their feedback. How do they define the authentic you? What is the great, the good, the average, and the yet to be developed for you? All of it. All of you.

Feedback can be generated through a formal 360-degree feedback process. Feedback can be easily gathered using index cards that are handed out and asking for words or phrases that describe the leader's actions or behaviors. It can be from a one question anonymous survey sent out to a group of people. It can also result from sitting across the table from an individual and asking, "What can I do as leader to help you be more successful?" When leaders ask questions such as, "How did I do?" or "Was that OK?" it does not extend the olive branch for truth. It asks for an affirmative response. Feedback is the desired outcome, not an affirmation.

If the individual across the table responds, "I would change nothing about your leadership style," challenge them. Challenge them to come up with one change, one gesture, one word, that would make a difference. If they are still hesitant, make a deal. "I will tell you one thing you can do better if you tell me one thing I could do better." Little doubt they will find something because now their actions, words, and behaviors are also on the table. Eventually, you will find those trusted advisors who will provide you with candid feedback that is meaningful. Treasure them. They may be one of the best learning opportunities you will ever have.

If a leader is not comfortable in his skin, well, the reasons could be many. And it could go back years and years. Looking externally for ideas may be the chosen route because they just can't find themselves, or the discomfort of who they are is too uncomfortable to face. They certainly are not going to be comfortable asking for help finding their own leadership style. So they look externally. Which leaders do they respect? What did they do? How did they act? What did they say? That external search scans the business world or history books to find a great leader to emulate so that they can become great too. It doesn't work like that. Various leaders have attempted this approach. It does not solve the problem. It is only a temporary Band-Aid and an ineffective one at that. It does not offer the opportunity for growth and development to be an authentic and respected leader. The inability to ask for help has been the demise of many leaders over time.

The best way to be an authentic leader is through self-awareness and having an appreciation for who one is as a person. Every experience, positive and negative, and every learning moment all matter and make leaders who they are today. If leaders do not like what they see, it is time for them to get to work.

Unfortunately, a great title does not automatically create a confident leader. A title does not eliminate the discomfort of not knowing all the answers. The fear of being found out as a fraud is an underlying fear. Apprehension of letting others know that you don't have the answers is an underlying cause for not making decisions. Arrogant behavior might be used as a method to create fear in others so they don't ask too many questions. The imposter syndrome may be at work. Finding a leader to emulate might be the chosen path if one lacks confidence, and it would be great if it were that easy. Hiding behind the facade of another great leader's image only works to slow down the development one needs to be a great leader.

LIFT. SWIM. EAT.

Each day, elite athletes begin their daily regime of stretching, conditioning, and training. Professional swimmers may start their day with weight training, then off to the pool for a few hours of swimming. The afternoon is back to the gym for more conditioning and more swimming. They will endure painful massages, physical treatments, and immersion in ice-cold water baths. Each day they rise and do it again. They train for the future. They know it is a journey.

The drive that keeps them going every day is their quest to be a champion. They endure the daily pain and discomfort. They give up time with family and friends to pursue their dream. As hard as they work, there's only one swimming phenom. It doesn't stop the others from working hard each day to be champions. They aren't trying to be the reigning champion. They are focused on becoming the best version of themselves with a goal of beating the current champion. They are inspired and challenged by the success of winners. However, they don't wake up each day and look to be someone else. They desire to be the champion that inspires others.

"Leadership is a muscle that needs development over time," shared one HR executive. "Like an athlete, one doesn't wake up one morning and become an Olympic champion that day. It takes time, dedicated practice, direct coaching, honest assessment of metrics, and continuous learning. The same is true for leaders."

YOU MIGHT BE A LEADER IN TRAINING

Being labeled a leader creates a "leader-in-training." People become leaders when they look over their shoulders and see a team willing to follow them and be ready to take on the next adventure. Until then, they are leaders-in-training.

"You want followers?

Focus on success.

Create incredible adventures that make others curious."

- Barbara Wichman

Everyone has their definition of leadership. This is my favorite definition because it reflects a leader who has developed trust, engagement, and employees look forward to what is coming next. Followers want to be a part of something greater than themselves.

Leaders sometimes forget that titles do not build instantaneous followers. Leaders have followers because of their characteristics and capabilities. Being a "crack-the-whip" leader results in compliance, not followers. Reaching goals does not make a leader great.

Being a leader-in-training is a great place to be. Capability and potential are recognized. But in all honesty, great leaders are always leaders-in-training. They define themselves as continuous learners. It is not a sign of weakness, it is a sign of confidence and strength.

Ask yourself:

- Are you comfortable with your leadership style?
- How do you define yourself as a leader?
- How do you want to be as a leader?
- Are you comfortable asking for truthful feedback?
- Are you aware of your leadership strengths and development areas?
- Do you readily engage in self-development?
- Are you a leader-in-training?

CONSIDER:

• **Being your authentic self may seem like it is not good enough to be successful**. If that is the case, the best path is to look for areas to develop rather than adopting a persona for yourself and try to present an image of a leader you are not.

• **Leadership is a muscle**. It needs to be developed like any muscle if you want it to be working at its highest potential. That requires developing awareness from 360s, coaches, and those trusted advisors who will tell you the good and the ugly.

• **Being given a leadership title puts you in training mode**. The work has just begun. For great leaders, their development work is never finished.

CHAPTER SIX

TRIGGER POINTS

WHAT IS YOUR TRIGGER?

One morning, 30 leaders were attending a session. The presenter was speaking, and at one point, one of the participants took his pen and threw it onto the table in what looked like a reaction of disgust. This reaction happened every time the presenter went into a story about themselves and their achievements. Because the presenter was engaging, most of the room listened to the stories with interest or, at least, tolerance.

During the first break, the presenter commented on the individual not paying attention. A guest responded that this participant, who the guest had been observing from the back of the room, had the same reaction each time the presenter migrated to a story about themselves. The presenter immediately reacted with some disparaging words about the participant.

Two individuals. Two triggers. Two distinct and visible reactions. Neither reaction was expected. Neither was productive.

Everyone has a trigger. It may be something big or something minor that invokes a reaction. Some have a long fuse line to reach the trigger. The level of reaction is different depending on the person. The reaction could as simple as the rise of an eyebrow or directing a gaze downwards. Or it could be more visible such as tossing a pen, sitting back in a chair and adding a heavy sigh. It might be a raised voice, pounding on a table or face turning red. Everyone will take notice of any leader's reaction and interpret the message it sends. Reach a trigger point, and the reaction is soon to follow.

Any reaction by a leader will be duly noted and shared. They may have an adverse reaction to a subject and therefore described as having a "touchy subject." Likely, this will generate warnings to others that may sound something like this, "Whatever you say, don't bring up the last project. I heard he went nuts!" Or, "No matter what the reason the project tanked, do not bring up the fact that the suppliers failed to deliver on time. I heard he screamed at the last person who brought it up."

In one situation, a leader was well known for giving a wink. Give a presentation, get a wink. Walk down the hallway, get a wink. One day, someone who received the wink asked a friend, "I got a wink when I walked from the front of the room. What the heck does that mean?" It was a good question. The wink triggered a reaction.

No one knew what the wink meant. It might have been the highest praise or just a greeting. The point is that some action triggered a wink. The wink triggered a reaction. So here was a person wondering what it all meant. No one knew but the winker. No one wanted to ask what the wink meant. It was confusing.

Whatever the reaction may be, employees are going to assess and interpret that reaction. It might be spot on, or it could be entirely all wrong. If it is entirely wrong, it could be disastrous for working relationships. It may cause actions that are counter to what the organization needs to be successful.

If you have ever been in any kind of relationship, you will most likely have your own example of a misinterpreted reaction and the subsequent fallout. It happens all the time. A work environment is not exempt from the perils of human interaction.

For a leader, misinterpretation can be detrimental to team work and goal achievement. If employees begin acting differently in your presence, dig in deeper to understand. There is a good chance your observed behavior, or your chosen words, are being interpreted incorrectly. The interpretation is causing them to shift their relationship with you. Find out now before the relationships get too far off track.

BAD REACTIONS

Leaders may have triggers that may cause them to react with intense emotion. Those around the table will lean back in their chairs or push back from the table to create distance between them and the reacting leader. Now everyone is focused on the trigger and the reaction. The natural response is to distance oneself. The impact is a derailed meeting and strained relationships.

Have you ever been in a meeting where a leader erupted? Yelling, swearing, and pounding a fist? Some may call the reaction passion. It is not passion. It is a leader that lacks emotional regulation. It is a leader that does not believe they need to treat others with respect.

A while back there was a sitcom that was set in a bar. The characters all had unique personalities. One waitress was known for her sharp tongue and hot-headed reactions. Her sharp tongue got her in trouble, so she had to seek help for her anger issues. They uncovered her triggers and helped her to see them. She was taught to go completely blank when facing her triggers, to numb herself. She was sent back to work and all the other characters tested her. She would go into a catatonic state to prevent herself from reacting. Leaders may not need to go to those extremes to regulate emotions, but there are tools and techniques that can be powerful. Coaching and feedback are the barometers to determine if the techniques are effective. Of course, the waitress in the show had to return to her old ways, or the show would not have been as funny. In leadership, there is no returning.

Any uncontrolled emotional reaction can stop truthful information flowing to the leader. Who wants to be the messenger of news that will cause a leader to flip out? Decisions are now impacted.

Relationships are strained. Trust erodes, and the culture suffers as a result. A leader's best offense when it comes to understanding their own triggers is self-awareness. Self-awareness requires honest feedback and truthful observations from others. Techniques to overcome triggers and lack of self-regulation requires coaching. Sustaining new behaviors requires feedback. It is one of those things that will not be successful trying to make changes solo.

A LEADER'S REACTION

There are essential tools used to provide individual leaders with feedback on how they are perceived. The tools were mentioned briefly previously, but it's time to dig in a little more. If you have not heard of the 360-degree feedback tool (360), it is an opportunity to gather anonymous feedback using a structured survey process. Input is requested from direct reports, managers, peers, and clients if so desired. The survey asks the same questions of all respondents and the summary of the answers provides insight into how leaders show up during their interactions. The 360 method requests commentary on strengths, development areas, along with other general comments. The 360 organized feedback is valuable for leaders to understand their impact and how they are perceived. The 360 outcomes can reinforce what leaders already believe about themselves, supporting their own self-assessment. The more valuable outcome is identifying any blind spots. Lacking self-awareness of certain behaviors or perceptions create leadership blind spots. Those blind spots have the potential to plunge the organization into crisis.

The 360 can be a jarring snap to reality. One shared comment may be the "bee in the bonnet" of a leader. There are times when leader is so incensed, they want to know who made a specific comment. They want to know who would dare to say such negative things about them. They demand to see each survey response and the respondent for each response.

One such 360 process triggered such a strong reaction in a leader. He was adamant the 360 vendor reveal all the responders' identities. If not all, at least the one who made critical comments. "I have to know who said these things. I am the CEO of this company."

The HR leader facilitating the feedback responded, "Because you are the CEO, you can't know who said what. If that information were to be shared, there would never be another 360 within the organization that would provide honest feedback."

Frankly, the damage would not be limited to just that organization. Ever so slowly, word would get out to other users that the confidentiality process of the 360 was breached and eventually no one would give honest feedback.

Organizations may also use engagement surveys, a method to obtain organization feedback on leadership and culture. If you aren't familiar with the process, once the survey inputs are compiled, the senior leaders get the first look at the results. After that, the results are distributed to individual leaders for their specific departments. The leaders are then expected to share the results with their employees to discuss and create action plans for improvement.

In one case, a statement included in an engagement survey result unnerved an admired leader. He demanded to know who made that comment. It was his trigger. He could not believe one person would say something so disparaging.

You see, everyone has a trigger point. The CEO, the admired leader, every leader has a trigger. Everyone has a perception of themselves, their values, their standards. They believe that others see them as they see themselves. They believe they live their values and standards every day. The problem is they are not always perceived as they believe. Interpretation of their actions can be different for each person. A leader never truly knows how actions or words are perceived, even with strong self-awareness. Leaders have no idea what goes on in the other person's mind. Considering all the people a leader may interact with throughout their career, someone is not going to like them for some reason. They are not going to like something said, a decision made, there will always be something.

Leaders need to learn to not let a comment result in an emotional meltdown. If there is one negative comment in an overall positive feedback process, the leader must discern how much emphasis should be placed on that one comment. On the other hand, if there are patterns in the results that indicate a gap between self-perception and the others' perceptions, there is a strong need to pay attention and make changes.

One HR leader shared that he fell into the trap of believing he was doing all the things that great leaders do. In his mind, he had it all down and, every day, he was leading the way great leaders lead. Yet each day, he felt himself struggling to be effective. It did not make sense.

After all, he was an HR leader. If anyone knows how to be a great leader, shouldn't it be an HR leader? It was not until he began to receive honest feedback through an extensive 360 process, that he was able to come to terms that his intentions were not the team's reality. It did not take long for him to make the appropriate adjustments and his daily effectiveness returned. Sometimes leaders don't know. They are completely unaware. Employees cannot always assume that the leaders' actions are intentional.

The value is in knowing there is a gap and knowing where the gap lies. There is no value in knowing who made remarks. Knowing the source only goes to serve the ego of the leader.

THIS IS NOT YOUR HOME

Leaders may become so comfortable in their role, their sense of their priority and privilege of leadership overshadows good judgment. They will do and say things even after advice is given to avoid an action or to stop. Even with coaching and feedback, leaders have been known to say, "I don't care. I am doing it anyway." They become so comfortable in their role they begin to treat the place of employment with the same sense of ease as if they are in their own living room. The workplace is not home.

Employees hear leaders make comments about people with disabilities. "Did you see he had two hearing aids? How can we hire someone with hearing aids?" And yet every company posts non-discrimination statements. Comments are made about applicants and employees ages. "Too young." "Too old." They use age to infer whether the candidate truly has the capabilities to do the job. Not enough experience if too young. Not able to learn if too old.

The list goes on and on. Legal lines are crossed. Because they are so comfortable in their role, leaders speak freely, too freely. Leaders may believe that making comments behind closed doors ensures confidentiality. That not upholding the company values is okay if no one is watching, or if surrounded by "trusted" people. They believe a closed door means private. However, it is never truly private. Comments are always overheard. And all is well and good until one comment rubs one person the wrong way.

These comments place the organization at fiduciary risk and, depending on the situation, personal financial risk. One of the most arrogant things that can be done as a leader is to put the shareholders' money at risk by violating rules and values. They become so comfortable in their work surroundings, they treat their workplace as if it is their home. They believe they can do as they wish, with no consequences.

Some leaders will comfortably make crude or derogatory remarks about how people dress, where they live, how they live, what they eat, drink, and more. Although this may not violate the law, it certainly may trigger reactions in those around them. It may cause them to be seen in a less favorable light. It erodes trust.

Leaders surround themselves with people they believe would never repeat the information shared behind closed doors. There is sometimes a sense of being able to say what they want because of their title. That is until the trigger of one of those in attendance is tripped. Now all bets are off. The sharing begins beyond that closed door.

Leaders of companies represent so much to so many. They represent their business in their industry. They represent themselves in community engagement and networking activities. They represent leadership. How they present themselves to others, causes the formation of opinions on leadership.

Leaders are human first. They will make mistakes as all humans do. But they must clearly understand that because of their role, their visibility is widespread, and the reactions to their actions and words are magnified. We expect more of leaders. Leaders are held to a higher standard.

LONG HAIR IS A TICKET TO HEAVEN

One day a fellow leader stopped in to say hello. He was tossing an orange up and down in his hand as he leaned against the credenza. "You know the Bible says that women should have long hair and not cut it short," he said out of the blue. The woman he was speaking to looked at him quizzically and said, "What?"

He continued with the profession of his beliefs. "Women should not cut their hair short. It says it in the Bible. If a woman cuts her hair short, the Bible says she will not go to heaven. My wife has never cut her hair." The woman could see others hanging around outside her door after hearing some of the words he said as they walked by.

"Thank you for stopping by. On behalf of all the women with short hair, thank you for letting us know that these women are not going to heaven. And you just got promoted. That's simply amazing."

"Thank you," he replied with a smile. Understandably, that phrase went entirely over his head. He believed it was a tremendous compliment. He took his orange and exited the door to continue with his new leadership role.

Leaders have triggers, and they create triggers. Leaders have company platforms in which they reach hundreds if not thousands of employees in one fell swoop. They have many one-on-one conversations. Communicating as a leader is a huge responsibility with the need to consider the audience, the state of the company, and current events impacting society's "mood." It impacts how employees receive the messages. Unfortunately, one can never be sure that the messages are going to be received the way they are intended.

When something is said or done that offends employees, there is hope that feedback will go back to the leader as soon as possible so they can be made aware before more damage is done. When leaders trip the negative emotions of others, it can be devastating. Respect is damaged. Followers start to fall by the wayside. The talk around the cooler repeats the leader's words or actions over and over.

Interpretations of leaders' true feelings and genuine character develop over time. One wrong move and the good interpretation can be erased instantaneously. If there is a negative belief about the leader, it is strongly reinforced. The problem is, no matter how accurate or inaccurate interpretations may be, they become reality in the eyes of the employees. They will be next to impossible to undo. The belief in the organization, trust in the leaders, respect for decisions, they are now all on the line. The culture suffers.

The leader's response to honest feedback will determine whether work can be done to work on repairs. If there is a negative response to feedback, the behavior will continue, and employees will be frustrated. Or worse yet, the fear of retaliation causes everyone just to walk down the hallway with smiles, making the leader believe that all is good.

Leaders shutting down feedback because they don't like the message, are missing opportunities to grow themselves and their business.

WHERE DID THAT COME FROM?

Carter attended a personal development program offered over a long weekend. It was one of those weekends where you learn a lot, and then they invite you to join them for a more extended engagement.

Carter was invited by a friend who had been involved with the program for a long time. His friend knew the folks that ran it quite well. During one of the breaks, his friend came over and said, "I want you to meet Gary." Gary was one of the leaders for the development program. Gary was highly respected by those engaged with the program.

Carter turned to see Gary standing next to him. Gary smiled brilliantly and said with great joy, "Hi, it is so great to meet you! I have heard so much about you." Now, if you were standing there and Gary said "Hi (add your name here), it is so great to meet you! I have heard so much about you." You would most likely reply in return, "Hi Gary, it is such a pleasure to meet you." You might add another sentence about how great the program has been so far. And then you might add what beautiful things your friend has shared about Gary. Right? The primary exchange of two people meeting and showing respect for each other. You would at the very least, be cordial.

This one time, Carter had a reaction that surprised even himself. Carter looked at Gary, and said with a very flat voice, "Hi." Carter then turned on his heels and placed his back to Gary.

Carter's friend needed a forklift to pick his chin up off the floor. He was astonished that Carter had responded so curtly. He had never seen Carter act this way. Not ever. Carter knew he had reacted with extreme rudeness and he didn't care. His entire mindset was, "I don't like you. Not even a little bit." The break was over. Carter went back to his seat asking himself, "Where did that come from?"

Carter signed up for the full program, and he saw Gary regularly at meetings. Carter respected his knowledge and teachings. Gary was great at what he did. And although Gary was always gracious, Carter still had an ill feeling towards Gary. He could not figure it out.

One evening, Carter was sitting in the classroom and Gary began to speak. Suddenly, Carter sat straight up and gasped. "Oh, my goodness. His profile. He looks just like him. His mannerisms are just like his." The understanding came full force. Carter was watching all the images in his head come and go. He smiled. He understood.

Carter's mind was racing. Carter finally understood. Gary's facial profile and mannerisms were the same as a man whom Carter had interacted with for many years. Carter did not get along with this man at all. Then, like a window shade opening to spotlight the answer, it all made complete sense. After class, Carter ran to his group leader and told her about his revelation. Carter kept saying, "This is what we are learning. How we react to things, without understanding them fully. I have to tell him what just happened."

Carter's group leader was shocked. She had no idea Carter was having adverse reactions to Gary this the entire time. Carter was adamant he needed to share his revelation with Gary.

Carter's group leader looked him right in the eyes and said with a firm voice, "I am not sure you want to do that." Carter could not believe she was trying to dissuade him from sharing his epiphany with Gary. His big aha moment arrived and all he heard was, "I don't think Gary would take that well. I am not sure you should say anything." What?

Well, Carter did tell Gary. He told him the entire story. Instantaneously, the reaction Carter had to Gary all this time completely went away. Carter finally understood why he had a negative response to Gary.

Carter can laugh about it now, but in all those many months, Carter could never understand his reaction. Triggers can be completely subliminal. And unexpected. A voice. A mannerism. A silhouette. A scent.

Any of these can trigger an association or a memory and that association will dredge up attached emotions. Unless you are fully aware of the reason for the emotion, you may have no idea why your response is so strong.

That may happen to people reacting to you as well. Something about you may trigger a reaction in them. You can't control it. That is why before you judge someone, get to know them first. The feeling you have about them may be from an old experience that has nothing to do with them. Give them the benefit of the doubt. Give them time to get to know you. You may discover you have many things in common and a fantastic relationship may blossom.

But here's the deal, if you are walking down a dark street and you see a person that gives you a concerned feeling. Take evasive and defensive maneuvers! Consider the situation.

As a leader, understand your own triggers. Question the source of the reaction. And if someone is negatively reacting to you, have patience. They may have received horrible news that morning. You just never know what may have happened to trigger their reaction.

CONSIDER:

• **Be aware of your trigger points**. If you are not sure what they are or do not think you have them, it is time to engage your team in sharing stories and examples while you listen. No defending. No excuses. Just listen, learn, and plan a correction course. Ask the team to hold you accountable.

• **Where you work is not your home**. Guard your words and your actions as if you were under surveillance. Those you trust most will be great confidants until possibly one day, something goes wrong. They now may feel compelled to start sharing stories. Treat every interaction with respect and honor the values of the organization. As a leader, one of your most important roles is that of a role model for the values of the organization.

• **Follow the law**. One of the most arrogant decisions a leader can make is to say and do things that are entirely against the law which places the organization in fiduciary risk and therefore risks shareholder trust and investments. If there are no shareholders, consider the risk of personal liability. Once again, guard your words and your actions as if you are under surveillance.

• **An adverse reaction may be the result of an association with a memory**. Allow time to get to know the other person before concluding your opinion. The trigger may be anything. The reaction is real. However, it may be misplaced.

CHAPTER SEVEN

VALUES AND CULTURE

THEY'RE WATCHING YOU

"People are our greatest asset," has been the spoken and written word by leaders and their companies over a long period of time. It is written on websites and proudly hung on company walls.

One HR leader shared how a recent conversation began. "I picked up the phone from a store manager who just had a visit from a corporate executive. The first words out of her mouth were, 'This creep just did this in my store. What do I do?'"

Stating that people are our greatest assets is all too often countered with real life examples that indicate a whole different set of beliefs. There are good examples, yet they are overshadowed with bad examples. Examples include stories of executives, leaders at all levels, first-line managers, and employees. No one is exempt. Everyone can be part of an example.

Real life situations of negative treatment are shared widely, and the stories travel faster than a bullet train. This has a devastating impact on the culture. It impacts the reputation of a company. It strains employee loyalty. Those that already mistrusted the company now feel vindicated for their feelings. Those that wanted to believe in the organization, now question that belief. It all happens so quickly. Leaders must guard the culture like a valuable gem. It can take months, even years, to build a positive and productive culture. It takes just moments to dismantle it.

LET'S ALL LISTEN, SHALL WE?

Organizations may spend weeks if not months developing core value statements. Then, to ensure that core values are lived each day, they will develop behaviors around those core value statements, so everyone understands what they mean. The core values might be evaluated in performance management conversations. If the core values are still not observed in the culture, specific actions will be developed to "highly encourage" the development of the practice or skill for that core value.

One such company had developed its list of core values, and one of those stated core values was "listening." The primary outcome the executives wanted from listening was for ideas to travel up to leadership from everyone in the organization. They wanted to ideas on how to have better processes and better solutions. They wanted to uncover roadblocks and gather ideas for eliminating them. They were genuinely focused on reversing the top-down communication flow that had become the standard. They wanted the information flow from the front line to the top levels to be just as active.

Executives thought long and hard about ways to make this new core value actionable for everyone in the organization. After much discussion, their path to change was to require all leaders to hold meetings where their only job was to listen to feedback and ideas. The intention was to create an upward flow of ideas representing all layers of every department. All leaders were instructed to hold meetings, including first line managers. There was such a strong desire to see the culture clearly at all levels, stand up meetings for those starting their assembly line shifts were implemented.

These actions were identified as an important process to creating organizational transparency. The leaders would take all the ideas they heard and share those ideas at the next level meeting. The leader who had called the meeting had one job, to listen. They could ask clarifying questions, but there was no debate, no dismissal, of any ideas. Can you imagine the implementation challenge this was going to be? The plan was developed. Processes and tools were communicated. HR representatives went to all the staff meetings to explain the process and answer questions. This was a big deal. It was going to take a significant amount of time and resources to begin the process, gain momentum, and sustain the process.

The executive team finalized guiding principles for idea selection and implementation. They were looking at financials to find funding for potential projects as a result of this new initiative. They discussed how they would share the guiding principles, select ideas, and recognize the idea originators. The executive team was all in.

The overall reaction from the organization was an unequivocal thumbs up. Employees wanted to be heard. They were actively preparing to share their ideas. And so, it began.

Leaders scheduled their meetings. You could hear chatter about this new initiative in the lunchroom, staff meetings, and in the aisles. Employees' reactions were positive. There was some apprehension as to if it would last. Yet, you could feel a spark in the environment.

Within the mix of leaders was a mid-level executive who was actively involved in the core values development process, including the "listening" value. He obediently scheduled his first meeting as did all the leaders. He opened his very first listening meeting with this statement: "Here's what I need you to do."

At first, those in attendance thought it was a joke. They waited for the punchline. The waited for the shift to the listening part of the meeting. It never happened. The manager proceeded to share his task list and his expectations. He ended the session with, "This was a great meeting!" He stood up and walked out of the room. The attendees were dumbfounded. It never changed. The listening meetings became the transfer of tasks, to become owned by those in attendance.

Suffice it to say, the leader was not going to let this unique opportunity pass him by. One could not defend his actions by stating he misunderstood the intention of these meetings because he was on the planning team. This leader saw the opportunity to use the time to his liking.

Do you believe he told his superior that he had hijacked these meetings? Of course not. He proudly said he was scheduling and holding listening meetings. He said he was learning a lot.

There was tremendous fear around this leader. No one wanted to challenge him during the meeting. History clearly indicated that fear of a future bad review, a public thrashing, or any other demise this leader might bestow upon the one who pushed back was a distinct possibility. That leader knew it. No one would dare say anything.

Any person to report this leader's behavior to his superiors might incur devastating repercussions including career derailment. What if the superiors didn't believe the story? What if they did believe the story? Would this employee now have a target on his chest? After all, a leader who has been in a position for a long time is valued and trusted. How would the leader fight back? It felt like a no-win situation for everyone, except for that one leader.

Values are rolled out with great pomp and circumstance. Posters are hung around the building. The second slide of every presentation lists the core values to reinforce their importance.

Most leaders work hard to embed core values in their everyday actions. They discuss core values at staff meetings. They focus on internalizing the values for themselves. They believe in the values and their importance to the company's success.

Yet one leader decides that those values are not as important as his own agenda. It demonstrates lack of respect for the company. The rest of the organization may be working hard to live the values with leaders doing their part. However, if all leaders are not on board, everything is out of balance.

THE CONDUCTOR

If you have ever been to an event with an orchestra, you will not hear one section being louder than the other unless it is part of the musical score. The orchestra conductor keeps each section in balance. Any one section out of balance creates an unpleasant listening experience. If you ever had the fun of attending a grade school band concert, you understand the concept quite well. The young musicians are still learning the importance of balance. At the professional orchestra level, balance is expected.

In organizations where large-scale change is already a challenging endeavor, that one leader who does not support the core values becomes that one section in the orchestra that negatively impacts the outcome. The higher the leaders' rank in the organization, the more power they wield, the more out of balance the culture becomes. Those leaders are conducting only for their own purpose, not for the overall success of the company.

Leaders are put in their positions to act on behalf of the company, while leading their specific department or function to success. There are collaborative leaders who find this balance and understand both roles. Unfortunately, there are also those leaders who have one goal, to win. They can be very aggressive in their methods. They create imbalance.

In the "listening" core value example, why is it that not one person spoke up during the meeting to question the process? Why did no one approach the leader outside the meeting? Why did no one report this behavior to senior leaders or HR? Here's why:

- Fear.
- Fear of retaliation.
- Fear of a sliding performance review.
- Fear of being passed up for promotions.
- Fear of the many ways that a career can be negatively impacted by doing so.
- Fear of public humiliation.

The employees doubt the organization will stand by them even though they are doing precisely what the organization has asked them to do.

The result is silence. Suffering in silence. Fear gets in the way of communicating inappropriate behavior. Lack of action by senior leaders when the situation is brought to their attention exacerbates anxiety and fear. It diminishes the trust that employees have in leaders and the organization.

Executives wonder why cultural elements they have worked so hard to define are not materializing. There can be many reasons: Lack of communication, direction, clarity, reinforcement, and leadership support. They need all leaders to be on board with values, strategies, operations, and mindset. It is the only way to succeed in a highly competitive landscape.

Often, values are integrated into the performance management processes to evaluate whether the employees are "living the values." They are assessed on the expected behaviors associated with the value. Training classes may be developed to teach and reinforce the behaviors. In one company, when new values were introduced, meeting room names were changed to core values words. Instead of being called Conference Room A, it was now Listening Conference Room. Companies go to extreme lengths to communicate core values and to embed values and behaviors in all aspects of the organization.

Leaders will communicate examples of how the values and behaviors have positively impacted the company. Sharing these stories inspires employees to align and encourage them to keep on the values path. I'm not sure the meeting room renaming was very impactful, other than creating confusion while trying to find the newly named conference rooms for a while. It was creative and certainly drove visibility to the new core values.

I GOTCHA THIS TIME!

Hank, the plant manager, led a very successful facility. He was known for his knowledge. He was also known for his tyrannical behavior. Because he was very smart, he was difficult to catch. He would get into physical fights with plant employees. No one ever reported him. He threatened employees. He pushed people around in the worst possible ways. Employees truly feared him. Employees would not speak up. He was always able to step aside and let the blame pass him by.

One beautiful day, he was caught in the middle of a physical fight. Both men involved were going to be terminated.

Hank had created so much fear that a police officer was called in to stand by outside the door during his termination. The HR manager in the plant was newly hired. Even though she was nervous, she was determined to fire Hank. She had seen his behavior and had been on the receiving end of his threats. She wanted to show the organization that she was not afraid. She knew he was a bad guy. They all knew he was a bad guy.

The senior HR executive arrived at the plant. He, along with the police officer, stood outside the door in case the soon-to-be-terminated leader started acting up.

When Hank was told he was terminated, he stood up and flipped the table. The HR executive and police officer rushed into the room. Hank was described as acting like a caged wild animal. He was escorted out of the building with rage in his eyes. Everyone was on edge, yet also breathing a sigh of relief. Finally, the tyrant had been caught in the act and was terminated. The entire employee population at the plant was grateful. They anticipated a new plant manager who would be respectful and lead them without fear.

Two years later, it was learned that Hank had recently been convicted of murdering two people. The murders took place before he came to work at the plant. Hank had a powerfully negative impact on the employees in the plant. Employees knew he was a bad guy, they just did not know how bad he really was. His tyranny went on for years until he was terminated. This is an extreme case however, bad behavior cannot be ignored.

There were several other examples during my interviews with leaders where facility managers were described as unfair and mean. They were bullies. They imposed their own rules. They broke laws. Employees in the plant were aware and full of fear. Executives were aware. Other plant managers were aware. Why were they left in their positions? Their plant was making money. Their plant was outperforming the other plants. Profit over behavior. The outcome for a company is always to make a profit. If not, why be a for-profit business, right? However, at what cost?

If a company is willing to forego its core values for profit, then don't develop or promote values. Leaders lose credibility. Employees are frustrated. Companies lose good employees at all levels of the organization.

But if the plant is making money, what is the price of losing a few good employees? It depends. It depends on how influential they are. It depends on if they sat in critical roles. It depends if they have knowledge and experience that is tough to replicate. Employees seeing an exodus of good employees depart, makes them wonder if they should leave also. They wonder what is wrong. When good talent leaves, remaining employees become concerned.

In another example, a company repeatedly shared the importance and value of the people. Then, an executive publicly humiliated an employee at a company event. It was regarding family choices the person had made, comparing the employee to someone else in the room who made a different family choice, a choice the executive agreed with. The topic had absolutely nothing to do with business. The employee's manager approached the executive to help him realize the negative impact on the employee. The reaction from the executive was anger. The conversation ended quickly. There was fear of retaliation or the potential derailing of the targeted employee's career. It happens all too often.

Leaders who do not uphold their companies' values and beliefs come in all shapes and sizes. They walk the hallways, smiling, believing they are not held to the same values, ethics, and laws as the rest. Some do not recognize that their actions are violating the values. Some know they are violating values and laws, and do not care, believing their title provides them with special privilege. Other leaders promote and actively live the values each day, admired by their teams and the organizations for their alignment with values, ethics, and respecting the laws.

Employees are watching. All the time.

The actions of a leader are dynamically louder than any stated words. Their actions will impact and evolve the culture into what the employees see, not one that the company states it desires.

"We respect our employees and value them as our most important asset." These are commonly used words and leaders want employees to believe that this is what the leaders think and how they behave.

Employees share stories as fast as they can when it comes to company culture and misalignment of values. Chastising individuals in work meetings for personal choices. Verbally demoralizing employees in front of each other. Commenting on how people dress because it is different from themselves. Speaking of employees' errors behind closed doors, yet never approaching them personally. Verbally demeaning employees in front of customers. All are representative of the stories shared. No industry is spared.

Leaders carry the torch for their culture. Leaders are the ones who represent the organization to the employees. Leaders are humans with a title, and that provides them a platform to be seen and heard. Leaders must use this platform wisely.

IT WAS PICTURE PERFECT

Along the river sat a beautiful and stately home. On any given evening, there was nothing more gorgeous than the view across the river to the woods on the other side. The trees had been growing on both sides of the river for hundreds of years. Grand old oak trees guarded the river's edge. It could be described as a scene one might read in an old novel.

The owner of the house was a senior executive at a local company. He was gruff and had a reputation for being a demanding authoritarian type. Even though he was challenging to work with, he enjoyed showing off his grand home along the river to his colleagues. He decided to hold his next business meeting at his home, followed with socializing. This meant all the spouses were expected to attend. He wanted a caterer that would live up to his standards in entertaining.

A young man on his team knew exactly which caterer to turn to for this kind of event. He knew the owner personally. He was comfortable they would do a great job. He reached out to the caterers and they were very excited to support this event. The caterers knew most of the folks attending and had catered many of their events. They were excited to do their part to make it a great evening. It felt like a win-win all around.

The day arrived and the caterers were sent to the pool area to set up their tables. They were focused on every detail. Since they knew many attending the event, they wanted everything to be perfect.

As the caterers were setting up, the executive's wife walked out to the pool area and demanded the caterers wash all the patio furniture immediately. She did not care that they were there to serve food and beverages. She wanted the furniture cleaned, and she was paying them, so they better do it and now. She ended with, "You are the hired help."

Cleaning patio furniture was not in the caterer's contract. The catering owner was not pleased to have his staff treated with such disrespect. They washed the furniture. He was going to fulfill his obligation and create a great experience as his past customers were going to be there. He was not going to let them down.

That caterer refused to work for that couple ever again. The word got out about the demands of washing the patio furniture. How could this company employ a person that allowed others to be treated so disrespectfully? Those were not the values of this company. How could he be respected when he treated people that way?

Although it was the wife of the executive who made the demands, she was viewed as an extension of the executive. The way the executive treated others was the same as how his wife treated the caterers. It was no surprise to his team.

The words that leaders choose matter. Their actions matter. However, their actions carry more weight than any words they choose. The culture of the organization is driven and reflected by their actions and their words.

The flipside is the organizations with leaders that consistently uphold organizational values. They create a culture whose employees bleed pride for the company. The leaders whose values and actions are aligned with the company develop loyal and engaged employees. They work harder for the company. They get excited when the company wins. They work hard to make sure the company does not lose. They protect the image of the company.

Companies put all kinds of programs in place to drive engagement and encourage dedication to the success of the company. More evaluation of behaviors, perceptions, and gaining an in depth understanding of the relationship between two, might be a better first step. If you want engagement, be a leader others want to follow.

INCLUSION AND DIVERSITY

Inclusion and diversity are words often used when companies define their competitive advantage. They speak of making their organization better by recognizing and honoring differences. However, many companies continue to struggle with making this come to life.

One company includes a specific sentence in the diversity and inclusion portion of its website. It reads, "Disability is a strength." How does this company live these values? Here are a few ways that were shared with glowing pride:

- Recognizing and respecting the unique and special.
- Valuing the contributions and ideas of women.
- Supporting developmentally disabled children in the community.

The most astounding fact is that the respect and pride for this company was stated by an individual who does not work, nor has ever worked, for this company. All these observations were from seeing the impact in the surrounding community and from hearing stories from friends and acquaintances. Companies build their reputations as they work to value inclusion and diversity with visible and meaningful activities. The respect can reach far outside the company's walls, as in this example.

People watch what companies do. They watch decisions that leaders make. Employees, investors, customers, suppliers... they all are watching. As a leader, what do you want them to know about you?

I CAN SEE IT

Have you ever been fortunate enough to be near a body of water that is so clear you can see the bottom? Well, first, congratulations! It means you have been someplace awesome!

You probably noticed something besides the clarity of the water. The view looking into the water distorts the position of the objects in the water. As the light from above bounces off the object, the light rays are refracted as they move from the water to the air. The eyes and brain do not recognize the refracting and interpret the line of sight as a straight line to the object. It is not. If you reach in the water to pick something up, you must adjust your movement to compensate for the refracted view.

As the water flows, your eye catches different movement in the water. You have certain expectations about what you will see in the water. It is easy to confirm if you see vegetation, a fish, rocks, or a discarded can. You identify those things that you easily recognize. If there are things you can't quite make out, you may look to others to identify them for you.

Senior leadership's view of their company's culture can be a similar experience. If there was one point shared repeatedly in my interviews, it was that there is often distortion between what the leaders believe the culture to be and reality. Looking deeper and outward into the organization will expose a variety of subcultures within the organization, directly influenced by local leaders.

One large company worked very hard to change the perception of the company in the eyes of the employees, and with its customers. The corporate offices were vibrant with the new direction. The pride employees felt to be working in this company returned. There was a concerted effort to also change the perceptions at all the facilities across the country. It was no easy task. Slowly, it began to get traction. They heard stories that indicated positive change was in motion. The senior leaders believed the progress was very positive and therefore they were feeling great.

During one executive's visit to a store, he invited several employees out for lunch. It was a great opportunity to get feedback on the recent culture changes. As they were walking into the mall, the executive noticed each employee removing their name badges immediately upon exiting their store. The visiting executive calmly questioned the employees about the removal of their name badges. He discovered that store employees did not feel the beaming pride like those at corporate. He returned to the corporate offices with a message. "We need to stop waving the flag of victory until the stores have the same feeling of pride in our company as those of us working in this building." That gap might not have been uncovered without the trip to visit a store far from the corporate offices. It was only with that visit they realized much more work was required before claiming victorious outcomes.

What causes such a gap? There are many reasons. Here are a few ideas shared.

• Communications are written with a corporate office lens. They are not appropriately written for audiences such as field associates or remote locations. It is not purposefully shared, nor is there any follow-up to ensure the messages are received. There is no opportunity for two-way dialogue that alerts leaders that something is amiss.

• Expectations and descriptions for the expected new culture lack clarity.

• There are struggles for limited resources resulting in competition, rather than collaboration.

• Internal politics emerge. Politics have a very effective way of waylaying the intentional building of a culture. The constant maneuvering to understand who is in charge and whose agenda takes priority diverts attention and energy away from intentional culture development.

• The fight for superiority. Who will end up with the power? Who is expected to retain control? Who is going to emerge the winner?

• There are rules, and then there are the "rules," implied rules not written anywhere and not shared in new employee orientation. These implied rules are "discovered" by new employees over time.

• Leadership ego drives many unhealthy behaviors. Leaders have been caught lying, hiding the truth, or withholding collaboration if they believe another department will one-upthem. A leader's ego infusing a department in support of the leader's needs, and not the good of the organization, redirects efforts for intended culture development.

These examples are common reasons why the desired culture does not permeate the entire organization. In addition to communication gaps, leaders see the opportunities to gain more or guard against loss. They are competing to win for themselves. The culture needs are put aside to fulfill the leader's personal goals.

Leaders may forget they are hired by the company. They are paid to work for and in support of the company. Their role is to drive the company initiatives. Their paychecks are fulfilled by the company.

LOOKING FOR VALIDATION

Leaders look to validate what is happening with examples of what they see or hear. They will listen for success stories about the new culture, so they can "prove" that the culture is transforming. As in the name-badge story, a few stories influenced the leaders' perception of progress. They were not bad leaders, they were looking for evidence and they found it. They just did not look far enough.

Say a company implements new performance management (PM) process. As part of the new process, managers are expected to ask employees, "What can I do to be a better leader for you, so you can be successful?"

The leader is expected to record the actions in the employee's online form. During the next performance review, these actions become a part of the performance conversation. At each subsequent performance review, the employee will rate the leader and further the discussion of what support they require to be successful. The actions and the rating are then connected to the overall assessment of the leader. This new action becomes a part of the integrated performance management process.

This change intends to create a culture shift in the performance assessment process. A shift from a traditional process, where the manager completes the review with the employees' input, to include identifying the manager's actions to support the success of the employee. The change also includes the employee rating the manager's actions. This rating, and the ratings from all the manager's direct reports, feeds into the manager's performance review discussion. It is new and somewhat scary change for many managers. Many employees are also apprehensive.

In this scenario, a few will adopt the new process right away, believing it is a great new addition to the performance management process. Some will not adopt it at all. The majority will do it out of obligation with average results, until they feel some pain for not doing it well, or until there is a payoff for doing it well. After all it's new, different, and it's a change to the process. It is the change curve 10-80-10 distribution again.

Inevitably, there will be one or two examples of the new change where it works with unbelievable outcomes. Those positive examples are shared with the CEO, who will share the success stories at town hall meetings, department meetings, and in company communications.

The challenge is that executives may assume that with a few great examples, it is indicative of success. If subordinate leaders communicate that things are going well when they are not (which may never happen), there is a distortion of the truth. Executives think everything is going great, but it is not. They hold a distorted view from the misinformation provided to them. When this starts, no one wants to be the bearer of the truth if things aren't so great.

Therein lies the gap, that gap between what the culture is expected to be and what the culture is for the rest of the organization. For leaders to be effective at building change and sustaining culture, an undistorted and honest view of the culture at all levels within their organization is required.

There is one best way to do that. Get out of the office. Meet with employees from different departments. Travel to different locations. Talk to employees. Eat with them in the lunch room. It might scare the heck out of the local leaders, but you may learn an awful lot about what the culture is like for the employees in their location.

Leaders can only act upon the information that they have in their coffer. If their information is from others, who knows what the truth may be? Most folks will be honest, yet there is always a distortion when it comes to opinions. Everyone interprets what they see. Getting out of the office and seeing how the employees are doing their work, the state of the facilities, and the culture in which they work is essential for leaders.

PEOPLE GO THERE?

One facility was in a rundown building that was a perfect image of disrepair and neglect. Yet it was a facility that was used to welcome and train new employees. The money budgeted for annual improvements and repairs was consistently shifted to something "more important" by the senior executive.

The training staff was talented, dedicated, and focused on giving the attendees the knowledge and skills they needed to be successful. They had gone from year to year with the same thing, other projects were more important, money for their improvements was gone.

One day a new leader came on board. She visited the facility. She took photos. She shared those photos with other more senior leaders who were also new. They reacted to the images using words such as "crap," "awful," and "morbid." One asked, "People actually go there? That place is the first image we give our new hires? Are you kidding? I would leave and never come back."

It was suggested to put a desk at this facility and require the executive that continually shifted those budget dollars to work there every day. To use bathroom stalls where the doors had long since fallen off and were in such bad shape, they could no longer be reattached. To eat in the room where the trainees were required to eat, the same room where products were stored for training. To have to walk into the facility through the same doors every day where new hires gained their first impression of the company.

Being open to the truth and not dismissing validation of truth goes a long way for bringing truth to reality. What employees experience every day may be very different from the executive's experience who is looking at it through a spreadsheet line item lens.

The executive was not moved to the facility. However, the facility did get some money back to make some improvements. It was a beginning.

CONSIDER:

• **Leaders are the role models for company values and culture**. Alignment is expected, and when it is not, it is the hot topic of conversation throughout the organization. Holding all leaders to the same values and cultural norms come under pressure when profit achievement is on the line. Staying true to the values builds trust between the employees and the company.

• **There is always a culture**. Some people have said, "We don't have a culture." Sure, they do. It just may not be the intended culture desired by leadership. As a leader, you choose to intentionally build the desired culture of engagement and success that is best for your organization, or to allow the culture to evolve on its own, which may not be the culture that is best for achieving strategic goals.

• **A few stories of success are not indicators of organizational adoption of process and culture**. Don't get taken in by a few good stories. Go find out for yourself.

• **If you want to know what the culture looks like in the company, get out of the office and engage the employees**. Travel to the facility furthest from corporate headquarters and spend time there. Eat lunch in the cafeteria with employees. Bring your lunch if you must or, better yet, cater lunch for the employees one day while you are visiting. It will give you the perfect opportunity to mingle and learn more about the local culture.

CHAPTER EIGHT

FOR NEW LEADERS

MY FAVORITE QUESTION

I have to say, one of my favorite questions I asked during each interview was this, "What would you tell those who are stepping into a leadership role for the first time?" It was evident great thought had gone into their responses. I felt as though I could hand over the notes from this question to any newly minted leader. They would be ahead of the game with words of wisdom that are so meaningful for taking on a leadership role for the first time, yet rarely given much talk time.

Becoming a leader for the first time is such an exciting opportunity. It brings anticipation of things to come. It's a dream come true for so many. It's recognition for all the hard work and learning experiences. It's also a time of transition, and it can be scary for a new leader.

There is pressure when one becomes a leader for the first time. After all, leadership is a buzzword we begin hearing in grade school. It starts early. Leaders are important. We learn that in school, playing sports, and hanging out on the playground. Leaders are valued. Society tells us that. We talk about leaders. There are leadership class, books, and seminars. Everyone talks about leaders. So, to be one is very exciting, and there is a lot of pressure to be good at it.

How do you set the foundation for long-term success? What are the key components to make the transition from individual contributor to a leader? What is the first thing a new leader does besides call his/her parents to share the news?

THE FUNDAMENTALS

As an individual contributor stepping into a leadership role, the limited view of their world has now expanded. Responsibilities no longer are just their immediate environment. What do they do? The very first thing a leader needs to learn is how to manage the fundamentals. But what management skills are essential?

• **Learn the business**. Now is the time to learn about all the aspects of the department. Understand the roles within the function. It is next to impossible to lead people if there is a lack of understanding of the business. That is the first order of business. Making decisions and offering guidance without this knowledge will lead to mediocre if not disastrous outcomes.

• **Understand who supports, and is supported by, the function**. What are the interactions required to keep things running smoothly? Where are the intersections? Who are the key players that the department collaborates with on a regular basis? Take time to understand processes and the connections. It improves the effectiveness of problem solving and builds meaningful relationships.

• **Understand strategy**. Be clear as to how your department supports the overall plan. Understand the landscape in which your company operates. Who are the competitors? What are the markets served? What are the upcoming challenges? What potential changes may impact your department?

• **Know the people**. Read job descriptions and performance reviews. Have coffee meet-and-greets. Take small groups for lunch. Engage with your new team and ask questions. Then listen. Walk the hallways. Stop by employees' desks and say hello. Get out from behind your desk and engage. If it is a larger team, consider holding an assimilation process so they get to know you and you get to know them. It is important to begin building trusted relationships.

• **Communicate often**. Set up regular meetings. Share information. Provide updates. Respond timely to inquiries. Provide feedback. Offer guidance and observations. Be available. Ask questions.

• **Be knowledgeable of employees' goals, development areas, and career aspirations**. Review all the details in their performance management reviews. Look for all the areas that the employee could use support. Have a meeting and talk about what they need from you. Look for opportunities to develop employees based on their needs and theircareer aspirations.

• **Remember, it is okay to have fun**.

Learning how to manage first will develop skills necessary to be a better leader later. Getting the fundamentals down in the beginning creates time for the more appealing aspects of leading. Management fundamentals may not seem as exciting. The fundamentals feel tactical, because they are. Get these down first. Get the team behind you so they will follow you as you lead them to the next adventure.

LOVING YOUR LOLLIPOPS

Transferring the old source of recognition to a new source of gratification is a significant speed bump to becoming a successful leader. Those things that made a leader successful with lots of kudos in the past are no longer relevant. It is time to forget the old way for earning lollipops.

An individual contributor receives recognition for completing tasks, for sharing new ideas, and for being an active member of the team. It is much easier for an individual contributor to point to "a thing," and say, "I did this." That object could be a report, order fulfillment, days without problems on a manufacturing line, or a brochure design. It is much easier for an individual contributor to receive praise for a specific accomplishment. It is readily identifiable.

When becoming a leader, there is a period where the pats on the back for a job well done are sparse. It is not because the leader is not doing a good job, it is because the source of recognition has now changed. That lack of attention is so hard. As humans, we crave it. We want to feel acceptance. Recognition and kudos provide that sense of "I am accepted. I matter. I belong." That is the fundamental need of every human being. It is what the brain looks for. And if it is not received, fear moves in. Feeling like being outside the perimeter of inclusion where it used to feel so good, creates pain and fear. What happens? Leaders look to return to those things where they used to get positive feedback. They are looking to fulfill that craving for those lollipops they used to receive with the things they knew how to do best.

Wanting lollipops does not mean the leader is unskilled, incapable, or has low emotional intelligence. What it means is that the new leader is entirely human. And most new leaders do not get the appropriate support required as the make this transition. They aren't given a handbook or good coaching on what the change feels like or how to manage their internal reactions. Everything is focused on the achievements that got them to where they are, and expectations for their future success.

As a leader, gratification now comes from servicing others. Creating an environment for team success is now the essential role. For a new leader, this can be very difficult to digest. They may intellectually align with the new role of gratification in their professional life, but that does not minimize their intense desire for the previous level of recognition.

New leaders may begin to believe that things are not going well, when things are going quite well. The transition can be challenging, and the new leaders may not understand why they are feeling so frustrated. When they are feeling like things aren't going well because of the lack of kudos, it is essential to talk to their immediate supervisor or reach out to their HR professional. It probably is going great. It's just that the lollipop vendor has changed, and they are still trying to find business with the previous vendor.

PERCEPTIONS ARE REAL?

"I was chosen as a leader because I'm great, right?"

"My team will admire me because I was chosen for my skills and expertise, right?"

"Everyone is glad I am their leader, right?"

Perhaps? Not necessarily. Most likely they will take a "wait and see" approach. New leaders get chosen for a variety of reasons. One reason is their past success in their individual contributor roles. They have proven their capacity for getting things done and recognized as being good at what they do. High ratings consistently over time, likability, and exhibiting leadership tendencies are evidence that individual contributors are ready to take on leadership roles. They are someone who can grow into a great leader.

Current leaders assess employees by comparing them against their own their strengths. They evaluate whether the person will fit in and be like them.

"He's one of us. He should make a great addition to the team."

"He's a great guy."

"She thinks like us."

"She knows the business like we do."

"I like her."

"I like him."

The individual contributor is chosen to be a newly minted leader.

So, like any normal human being, there is a desire to do what you know, do it well, and receive recognition for your achievements. The internal struggle begins. The perception that a new leader may perform well because of past success is typical. The opinion that someone who thinks like us will make a successful leader in the future is not correct.

It is crucial for a new leader to see themselves as a leader, but through the eyes of others. The transition process requires loads of self awareness. Self awareness is something new leaders don't always have. A new leader may be doing all the things they have been coached to do, read about, and observed in other leaders. As they implement all their great ideas, that "greatness" may be landing with employees in an entirely wrong way.

Rather than letting animosity, agitation, and irritation build with a team and peers, it is essential to check in early and often and see if reality is playing out the way it is thought to be.

There are many available tools for obtaining unfiltered feedback. The 360-surveys have a few weeks turnaround timeframe. However, new leaders need quick and simple feedback mechanisms.

The simple index card exercise is an option at any staff meeting. Provide everyone an index card and ask your team to write down three words or phrases to describe you as their leader. Have someone collect the cards confidentially and provide them to you. The value is in the feedback. Stop trying to match penmanship.

Another quick option is to deliver an anonymous survey with one question. "Please provide three words or phrases that best describe how you perceive me as a leader." Everyone can respond no matter where he or she resides. You can have two surveys, one for your team and one for your peers. If the numbers are too small and anonymity cannot be guaranteed, combine them. There are companies that provide quick and free surveys.

The hardest step, no matter what method is employed, is to share the outcome of any feedback back to the team. Ask for ideas and specific actions based on the feedback on how to be a better leader. It is much easier to have the discussion as a new leader. People are much more forgiving of new leaders. They aren't expected to be perfect or know all the answers. Unfortunately, a new leader may be very nervous to ask for feedback. It is uncomfortable but worth the effort.

If being the best leader possible is the goal, then openness to unfiltered feedback to correct any fledgling misperceptions is a positive first step. HR can assist in facilitating the conversations. HR professionals are typically skilled in facilitation.

BUILDING LEADERSHIP MUSCLE

Building leadership capability is like building a muscle. It takes time. It takes repetition and focused attention to develop any muscle. It is the same for leadership.

Athletes focus on developing muscles. More specifically, athletes develop what is called "twitch muscle fibers." Football or volleyball athletes develop the fast twitch muscle fibers for explosive jumps and speed. Long distance endurance athletes develop slow twitch muscle fibers to allow them to complete long distances, like marathon running. Fast muscle development is a not valuable for endurance athletes. Slow twitch muscle fibers would have little benefit for athletes requiring quick reactions and repeated power bursts. The point is that emphasis on muscle development is specific and intentional. There is a laser focus on developing the skills most relevant for success.

New leaders are developing their muscles. New leaders have much to learn. They need to be fast in some areas, but slower and more deliberate in other areas. Development should focus on the capabilities that will support their success, short-term and long-term.

New leaders are not always sure where to focus their time and energy for development. What should they develop first? How many competencies are there to choose from? Which one should they select? Who will lead their development? How will they know what development area is most critical for their current needs? What about future needs?

There are two great places to look. One, start with the current situation and a hold a discussion with the new leader's manager. What are the competencies necessary to lead right now? What are the immediate concerns that the leader will be facing and what development can be realized?

Two, look at the feedback from the index cards or survey exercise. Most likely one or two areas for development will show up. A new leader does not need a leadership development course right away. What the leader needs is some simple feedback to focus on a couple of key areas. The direct manager, HR or a mentor can provide coaching feedback. Don't overcomplicate it. On-the-job training is some of the most effective learning ground there is, if there is a good coach to guide the way.

Great leaders continue to build and refine their leadership muscle. They believe the need for continuous learning never ends. The number of skills that require development may be fewer. There is focus on refining skills already in place, as well as new skill creation.

Developing as a leader is a journey over time. Leaders get better and great leaders never stop improving. Leadership endurance builds over time. Leaders must be patient.

BE OF SERVICE

One of the chosen "most admired leaders" was President Dwight D. Eisenhower. Before his presidency, he was a five-star general in the United States Army. He served as Supreme Commander of the Allied Expeditionary Force in Europe. He was a highly respected leader. His role was being of service to others for the overall success of the country.

Descriptions of his leadership style included confidence in himself and others, courage, humility, and the ability to make decisions. He had developed and exercised his leadership muscle over a long period. He was not reactionary. He was responsive. He was a great planner and he executed plans intentionally and thoughtfully. His leadership was always in service to others.

New leaders must develop the courage to serve others. Tony, who was pressured to step away from all agreed upon work streams and focus his entire team on completing an urgent request from one leader, stood in a moment of truth. He could walk away from his service to the greater organization to fulfill this one project. One leader made a unilateral promise to another leader, without consulting the rest of the organization, and wanted previous commitments ignored.

Tony's courage to say no, even under the threat of insubordination, was an example of service in leadership. He risked personal hardship for himself and difficulty for his team. He was told directly, "you must do this." He said no. Tony had committed to the greater good of the organization, and it was the service he was going to fulfill. His courage to say no exemplified his dedication to the many, over the misstep of another leader who was trying to save face. He had leadership muscle. He understood what service truly meant.

As a new leader, now is the time to learn to love serving others. Time to learn to have the confidence to hire people better than you. With that confidence, great accomplishments are within reach. Learn to tap into all the diverse skills and ideas. It is not always easy to surround yourself with employees who know more than you. However, that is the way great leaders move mountains. They are not afraid of being wrong. They are not afraid of not being the expert in the room. They see value and growth in everyone participating and sharing their experiences.

New leaders are starry-eyed with hopes and dreams about all their future achievements. Successful outcomes require the team behind the effort. New leaders need followers. Followers are created by servicing the highest needs of each employee and supporting their growth and success. One of the most significant accomplishments a leader can have is an amazing and successful team.

Your team is not of service to you. You are of service to them.

It sounds easy. It's not so easy to execute. New leaders have opportunities to make a difference. They are rarely confident in how to do that as a newly minted leader. It takes time. There will be missteps. Each misstep is a new learning opportunity.

FAILURE IS NOT FAILURE

Being a new leader is such an exciting time. Days are filled with hopes, dreams, and pride. Learning to love what leadership is all about creates opportunity for a long term and successful leadership experience, not only for the leaders, but for all those that work for and alongside them.

The role of leadership is not for everyone. Not everyone succeeds at being a leader.

Becoming a new leader and hating it, is not a failure. Being chosen to lead and failing is not a testament to the value of the individual. Too often, recognizing that the newly appointed leader should remain as an individual contributor is viewed as a failure. They often feel attacked, frustrated, and abandoned. Once relieved of the responsibility, there is a good chance they will feel a sense of relief. There's no failure in a role not working out. There's no shame.

Why might new leaders fail?

- They never wanted the role but were afraid to turn it down.
- They do not like it.
- They lack support and good coaching.
- They have ineffective management above them.
- They do not receive feedback.

There are so many more reasons. Each situation is different. Some are just not good at it. They have other gifts that will make them successful and feel valued.

ONE GREAT PUTT

There is no doubt that leadership is a tough and a rewarding role. It is not always lollipops and sunshine, but some moments will swell the leader up with pride. It is those moments that keep the leader moving forward.

It reminds me of my dad who loved golf. It was his life passion. Even as a consistent golfer, there were shanked shots, many sand traps, and shots that ended up too long, or way too short. However, it was that one fantastic putt. That one amazing drive that when the club connected with a ball, he just knew it was awesome and he would smile. It felt great. Leadership is kind of like that. One great shot or great putt is all that is needed to sustain the drive to keep building that leadership muscle. There will be amazing moments when you know you did it just right.

WISDOM FOR NEW LEADERS

For a newly minted leader to make a successful transition from individual contributor to a successful leader, five lessons emerged.

1. **Learn to manage**. Get the fundamentals down so you can focus on developing leadership muscle.

2. **Ask questions and listen to everyone**. You will learn so much more than if you fill that time telling everyone about yourself. Learning is the outcome of hearing what others share. It increases understanding. Listen to what is said and what is not said. Listen to what employees are saying in your immediate location. Make a concerted effort to get to the front lines and listen there as well.

3. **The source of gratification needs to shift**. This shift may result in loneliness and agitation because the kudos don't flow as they used to in the past. Recognize that the very nature of the work has changed. Therefore, the recognition will come from different activities. New leaders make mistakes. Rename them "learning moments" and move on.

4. **The leadership role is to be of service to others, not vice versa**. Stand firm in service for the good of the organization and do not allow individual agendas to take the work off course. Have the courage to say no. Find your brave heart.

5. **Opt for a reality check**. Use feedback mechanisms to check in with teams and peers. There is a chance the leader's actions may be interpreted very differently by those around the leader. Being able to tap into the truth will allow for early course corrections. Ask for examples and observations.

One final thought on new leaders. Employees are also going through an adjustment phase with new leadership. Consider an assimilation process to reduce the length of time it takes to discover each other. It will allow for a more effective transition for all.

CHAPTER NINE

THE PEOPLE

Employees love to learn about their leaders. That is why they observe everything leaders do. The more leaders can be vulnerable and share truthfully about themselves, the more significant connection employees feel with their leaders.

THIS BLOG IS ABOUT ME

The function was indeed global. There were employees in large cities, rural areas, and remote locations around the world. The team supported each other. They asked questions and looked for ways to assist each other. Whether it was understanding local laws and customs, researching technical issues, or connecting each other to locate the appropriate resource, the team was engaged. There was genuine respect and admiration for one another.

However, like large global teams, there was a disconnect with the senior leader. He traveled extensively, but could not possibly get to meet everyone personally. The team members wanted to feel a stronger connection with him. He was charismatic and friendly. So many felt like he was just a name, a shadow, not a person, and primarily an email distributor.

For the entire team to feel more intimately connected to the leader, the suggestion was made for the leader to write a blog. He was open, raw and shared his honest opinions. The leader was an excellent writer. The employees enthusiastically read his blogs. The feedback to the leader was, "love your blogs."

In these blog posts, he shared stories of his family, he wrote about his children, and he wrote about the excitement of what it was like to travel all over the world and meet fellow employees.

He shared news about the organization, such as leadership changes and the reasons behind organizational decisions. He wrote about new products and why they were essential to the future. He shared function success stories, and why it mattered to the rest of the organization. His blogs became a source of openness and sharing the function had never experienced before.

These blogs continued for several months. The function at large was able to gain a glimpse into the life of their leader. They learned of his intense passion for his family. They enjoyed his stories on the organization. The employees felt informed for the first time.

As with many companies, business was shifting, and the time came where the difficult decision was made to downsize. The leader continued with his transparency and announced that the function was going to be downsized 30 to 35 percent globally. It was a devastating blow. This department, although geographically dispersed, had become a tightly knit community over time. They liked each other. Relied on each other. They respected each other. Everyone was worried, not for themselves, but for his or her colleagues.

A few days after the announcement, the leader posted another heartwarming blog about his vacation with his family. The written descriptions were beautiful. It was clear that it was a fantastic vacation full of new memories. The blog was posted, and it took all of 30 minutes for the e-mails from around the world to start showing up in email inboxes. "What is this? We have over one-third of our population losing their jobs. He feels that now is the best time to talk about his expensive family vacation?"

The frustration and outcry grew louder as the day went on. Employees in the function were incensed. There were a few nice comments from a smattering of employees on the blog. Mostly, the reaction was anger and astonishment at the lack of empathy by the leader.

A colleague approached the leader and explained the gravity of the reaction from the employees and the negative impact it was generating around the globe. "They asked to hear about me, so that's what I wrote," he replied matter-of-factly. "So, you're saying I should take the blog post down?" "Yes, it would be a good idea to take that blog post down."

Granted, this leader was correct. He had been asked to write the blog about himself, and he was generous in his sharing. He was honest, vulnerable and you could see his human side in the blog posts. He openly shared information about the organization. However, that one post. That misstep. That one post turned the blog into something ugly.

Every communication will have a different interpretation by the employee base. With any communication, an environmental scan is necessary to realize the potential impact. It does not mean a leader should not be vulnerable and not share. In this case, it was tremendously successful. However, the change in the organization caused an immediate shift in the mood of the function. It was time to shift the communication to reflect the recent announcement.

Leaders must always remain cognizant that how a decision impacts them, and how a decision impacts the rest of the employees, may be different. Consider the impact all the way to the front line.

EVERYONE MATTERS

As a leader, a lens on the landscape is always required. Determine if it is still the right time for the messaging. Because everyone matters. Every person matters. How they feel matters. What they think matters. Their opinions matter. They all make the organization successful by being excellent in their responsibilities.

If every Amazon delivery driver decided to walk out, what impact would that have on Amazon? What effect would that have on the company's success? They are the last link of everything that happens, to get that product in the hands of the consumer. They are incredibly important to the customer service experience.

If you walk the floors of Nordstrom's, you see beautiful clothing. You meet helpful sales associates ready to assist you with your questions or search for a specific item. You wander through the shoe department and you see a fantastic selection of styles and the latest trends. The barista creates a master mocha that you enjoy as you shop. You walk into the restroom. The floors are littered. The sinks are a sticky mess. The garbage is overflowing. It smells bad.

That one experience easily wipes away the perception of all the other images and experiences that customer had until walking into the restroom. The employee that maintains the restroom is as valuable as anyone else working in the store. I have never seen a filthy bathroom in a Nordstrom's store. Every person matters.

The greatest gift the leader can do for themselves is to travel to the far reaches of the organization and meet employees in their work environment or invite them in for a visit. Be completely aware of the entire service chain. A janitor with intense pride in their job is important. A sales associate who loves to help the customer find the perfect outfit is invaluable. The associate that remains patient and treats the customer as though they are the most important thing in the moment, is an incredible asset to a company. Make decisions as though there is no such things as "just an employee."

MAKE TIME TO MEET EMPLOYEES

Locally schedule time for open-door, drop-in visits. Scheduling time allows folks to know you are expecting their visit. Eliminate the "always open-door policy," that often results in a "Why are you interrupting me look?" virtually ending the benefit of the open-door policy. Be accessible. Eat lunch in the cafeteria and join some folks you have not met yet.

If you are not sure where to begin, start with your high potentials and high performers. They are at the most significant risk for getting swept up by other companies. These two groups are also the ones who are looking for more challenge, for growth, and want to be fully engaged. Leadership interaction, finding the right projects for learning and growth, these are engaging opportunities for those that at highest risk for being lured away with promises of more challenging assignments and enhanced growth.

Whatever you do, get out from behind the computer and meet people. The effort alone will win you huge points with the employee population. They know how busy you must be. Employees appreciate the effort. As the leader, you must be the one to make the extra effort. Don't leave it up to the employee. Many believe you are not interested in them already. There will be the overzealous who want to take all your time and may end up irritating you to no end. Manage those that are overzealous. Let the rest know you are interested.

If they don't come to you, go to them. Organize coffee meetings with small groups of individuals. Ask questions. Listen. Learn about your employees, not just about their jobs, but about their families, interests and dreams.

One company implemented gatherings for the leaders and employees to build stronger relationships. The concept was the right idea. But the leaders spoke about themselves intently for a straight hour with a captive audience. Help leaders understand the importance of asking questions and engaging others in a conversation, not downloading themselves on the employees. Provide a list of questions if necessary.

Sure, there is a desire to learn more about leaders. But the effort will have much greater meaning if the leader spent time learning about the employees as well.

LEADERS ARE STEWARDS

Those under your stewardship require your care. That care includes high standards and productive dialogue. It includes chasing opportunities and providing a roadmap.

Being a leader is not being a friend. A leader must always be the leader. The employee you have made a friend and trust might also be the one to get the angriest with you if they don't get that promotion, that awesome project, or that raise. It might result in everything you shared with them in confidence now becoming your new nightmare.

Developing visible friendships with employees may leave others feeling left out. Pain from not being in the inner circle impacts behavior, engagement, and discretionary effort. Everyone wants to belong. Every employee wants to matter. The trust in leadership suffers. Is she now going to only value input from her new bestie? The leader-employee relationship is a powerful connection. Realize, though, that employees are not your friends. Relationships impact the culture and the organization.

Having to maintain professional relationships is one of the reasons why leadership feels lonely. It is not easy to spend a large portion of your day in an environment where you are not able to just be yourself, talk about your family, your challenges, your hopes and dreams. Leaders must always set themselves apart. They must be leaders, not looking to develop friends within their teams.

Leaders must remain neutral. They withhold judgment until they can get to know employees and provide their own assessment. Listening to hearsay may leave the leader with incorrect information.

Have you ever met a new person and your friend pulls you aside to tell you all about him? You trust your friend and her opinion. That information could be positive, or it could be negative. Usually, it is in the form of gossip. Unfortunately, this behavior happens in the workplace all too often.

The problem is that there are multiple points of view about any one individual. That one story you hear may be a fraction of the larger story. Those telling the story may have biases or other motivations to influence your perception. They may be intentionally looking to sway you for whatever reason. They may feel threatened by the other employee and see your friendship as an opportunity to gain the upper hand.

The leader's role is to learn about individuals and not engage in gossip and hearsay. Gossip is a dangerous activity in any organization. It completely steals time that can be used talking about productive topics. It destroys the opportunity to develop relationships before they even have a chance to form. It spreads rumors and negatively impacts collaboration, productivity, and trust. Those who generate gossip are looking to gain a posse to support them in whatever they are feeling. Instead, tell the gossipers to address the person. Have a conversation and align on a solution. Salacious gossip negatively impacts the culture. It drives mistrust and a game of "one upping" others, and only makes the gossiper look immature and difficult. Even worse is the leader who enjoys gossip.

Making the numbers is the ultimate outcome. But unless the company is run entirely by robots, the leader must be the steward for employees and the culture. The role of leaders is to balance the needs of the organization with the needs of the people, with a caring spirit. It takes constant negotiations and balance to make it work effectively.

R.E.S.P.E.C.T

The executive asked me to write a presentation for an audience of 100 business leaders. I was given no direction. I decided to set up a meeting to ask the executive what points he wanted to make. He was annoyed. I just wondered if there was anything specific he wanted to share. His response was to write it down and give it to him. He would tell me if it was good or not.

I worked on the presentation for a few days. I handed the executive the presentation. Without reading it, he threw it back at me. "It's not worth my time. Write something worth me reading."

This executive always made me feel like I had egg on my face. His preferred style was to put me, and everyone else, down. He liked to use zingers that would be insulting jabs. Everyone deferred to him. He would not allow anyone to fly on the corporate jet with him. He had to have the plane all to himself. His ego was massive.

Eventually, I learned to deal with it. I walked into each meeting and imagined the executive as a stand-up comedian. I would wait for it. Wait for the zinger. I made it a game. By treating it as a game, I was able to deal with his behavior.

In another situation, I had to make dinner arrangements for a senior leader who was flying in to address a new group of students. There were many rules for his travel. He must be greeted when he landed. He must have a welcome carpet provided when he exited the company jet. His feet were never to touch the tarmac.

He required special catering which included champagne where ever he stayed. I called his secretary to inquire what food he enjoyed. He would be landing late that evening, and it was important that he had a place to eat with the meal he required. His secretary said she had no idea what food he might want. I replied, "Can you ask him?" She could not possibly ask him. No one asked him that. "Have options for him," she said. "Make reservations and give him options."

As instructed, I had options. I reserved private rooms, a special menu, and an exclusive wine list, at three separate restaurants. I had made special requests for them to stay open later than their normal hours because this leader would be arriving after their regular closing time. Yes, he most likely ate a specially prepared meal on the plane while he was in flight. When he arrived, he would most likely be tired. However, he insisted that dining arrangements were made so he had options. In addition to the reservations, I stocked his condo with champagne.

He arrived. He went straight to his condo. I contacted all the students and sent them to the different restaurants. It was late, but they did not mind. I was not going to stiff the restaurants after all their preparation work. I told the students to enjoy the service afforded to kings.

These are stories of arrogance, pompous behavior, and having no respect for anyone. There isn't any connection to how their actions positively impact the company. Moreover, their actions wasted the company's resources. That doesn't show respect for the company or the shareholders from any perspective.

Always think about what kind of leader you want to be. Leaders that push employees around, demand special treatment, and then fail to acknowledge those that are working hard to satisfy those requirements, are blatantly disrespectful. Do you ever wonder what their mom or grandma would say if they knew the truth of their behavior?

IT'S A PAYCHECK

Too often, employees are viewed as a line item that requires financial management. Human resources are expendable resources. Sometimes it is forgotten that the word human is first. The churn and burn of employees are costly and time-consuming. It negatively impacts productivity, excellence, and that critical bottom line.

Remember this. The place of employment is an address and a paycheck. There are other addresses and other paychecks. Each day the sun comes up, the only thing that matters is that our loved ones and pets are excited to see us each time we walk in the door. Each day there are fewer reasons for people to stay where they are not valued. The leader's role is to create an environment where everyone is valued, engaged, and appreciated. The bottom line is people want to succeed. Treat them as such, and you may be amazed at the outcome.

CONSIDER:

• **Be aware of the current environment and the messages you are sending**. Be sensitive to what is happening in the culture. Things change rapidly. Emotions rise and fall. Allegiances shift. Make sure your messages are appropriate and not based on past values or expectations.

• **You are a steward of the people and the culture**. Care for the people as if they are your main priority. Avoid all forms of gossip and never let it be your guide. Get acquainted with the employees. Make yourself available for employee interactions. Get out of the office and visit other locations. Learn about your employees.

• **Above all, remember that every single person in the organization matters**. The job may seem trivial to you, but if the job is not completed well, the impact may be significant. Treat everyone with the utmost respect. Even the person that is emptying the garbage cans.

• **Show respect for others**. Your treatment of others is your leadership brand. Make it a respected brand.

CHAPTER TEN

UNDER THE MICROSCOPE

BEWARE OF PAPARAZZI

When you attend a new car show, you see the fancy new cars on a rotating platform with spotlights so that you can see every detail of the new vehicle. Leadership is a lot like that. Sure, there are going to be a few things under the hood that will not be seen, but everything else is visible and with bright lights illuminating every feature.

Leaders are on stage every day, wherever they go. People will watch to see what the leader wears, what they eat, how they interact with others, and it is all shared rapidly within the organization.

A new executive had joined an organization. No one knew much about this guy. All they heard was that he was considered brilliant and had a rich background. One day, after the new executive had been there for a couple of weeks, the notifications started coming.

"He likes coffee. He drinks a lot of coffee, but not the cheap stuff. He likes good coffee. He is married and has kids. Did you see his shirt? The brand isn't cheap."

So, what happened? People started to watch for him every day at the coffee shop. Men wearing the same brand of polo shirt began to appear in the hallways. Employees watch closely.

Leaders are on stage all the time. Employees watch what leaders do. They watch what leaders don't do. They observe decisions made. Employees listen intently to the words chosen. Words are interpreted, correctly or incorrectly. Discrepancies between what is said and actions are retained for future commentary.

Observation of whom the leader engages with a joyful morning greeting and discussion about the night before versus who receives a perfunctory "Good Morning" is stored in memory. Whom they sit down to eat lunch with or invite out for coffee is noted. Which desk they stop at and engage in small talk is observed.

Who's in the inner circle? Who is in and who is out? Most leader's waking time is spent commuting to and from work, at work, traveling for work, and engaging with others outside the office environment. Wherever there are employees around, leaders are being observed.

If the leader is in a crappy mood, word gets out. Stories swirl around the leaders. Assumptions are made. The stories may be true or false, but they are created. Once stories are formed, they are difficult to undo. Contrary evidence is dismissed. The leader's brand is developed. The leader is someone the employees enjoy discussing.

Now, if you were a leader in the 1970s and you streaked on purpose at a work function, you could only expect that people were going to talk about it. Don't try it today. You'll be led away in handcuffs and charged with indecent exposure. However, in the 70s, it was part of the national culture. They even wrote songs about the phenomenon. Today, people throw buckets of ice over their heads or pay it forward. Remember that if a leader promotes it, employees will participate.

As a leader, your employees are now your paparazzi. You may not see them, but they are watching you. They may not be taking your photo, but they are repeating your actions, decisions, demeanors, and stories to all the other employees. And they are adding their own commentary, as is everyone else. Like it or not, being a leader means being in the spotlight. Think of it as being on stage and the critics are always writing about you. You just may not see or hear what they are saying.

THE VIP IS HERE!

It's amazing the time and energy that is spent getting ready for a visit from a corporate executive. Stores spend weeks preparing for a one-day or half-day visit. Weeks of time, energy, and resources all putting forth the absolute best impression for that leader as they walk through those doors. The moment arrives. The leader walks into the building. What leaders do or do not do at that moment will define their brand instantaneously in the eyes of the employees.

Employees get dressed in their best outfits. They are ready in case the leader stops to acknowledge them. The leader may comment on their organized department. Everyone is on edge, nervously anticipating what the leader will say. Will the feedback be positive? Or will those keen leader eyes find something that is out of place?

Everyone is on their toes and in position. The leader walks in the door and without making any eye contact, walks directly to the meeting room. Employees work for weeks to get ready for this visit, and the leader didn't even stop to acknowledge anything or anyone as he or she walked through the store. The microscopic assessment begins.

How would you label those leaders?

Descriptive words like arrogant, non-caring, and self-absorbed, come to mind. What leaders forget is they are representatives of the greater organization. They are the company in the eyes of the employees. If people are our greatest asset, and we value contributions of all our employees, leaders that walk to the back of the store without even a hello receive an F grade. They may be lucky and get a D minus.

All leaders need to do to communicate respect for the employees, is to say "Hello! What's your name?" They can share thoughts about the department. "I can see the effort you and the team made. I appreciate all your efforts."

It is so simple to have a positive impact, yet some leaders are so blind to the opportunities. They are caught up in the importance of their own time and position. They forget that without those people selling products, ringing up sales, gathering the shopping carts, there would be no executive role to fill. There would be no meeting room at the back of the store.

Leaders get big kudos when they connect with employees while visiting remote locations. If the visit is intended to meet employees and share gratitude, the site will be a buzzing about the leader's visit. Employees will share how much the leader appreciated the employees.

Employees engage with companies when they feel they are valued. Those visits are opportunities to create a favorable view of the organization. It is amazing how much harder employees will work when they feel respected by visiting leaders.

As a visiting leader, be aware that your interest might generate fear and apprehension, especially if it is a new behavior. Local leaders and employees will wonder why they have been singled out for a visit. The job of the visiting leader is to ease fears, create goodwill, and leave those behind with a sense of pride and accomplishment.

YOU SCARE ME

I recall a conversation with the facility manager who asked me why I was unexpectedly visiting the facility. After all, it was a 45-minute drive. I was doing precisely what leaders are coached to do. Visit the facilities. Introduce yourself. Meet the people.

The facility manager was very concerned. I was HR. A drop-in visit from HR meant nothing good was going to happen. Was someone getting fired? The employees were nervously looking at each other.

The manager asked that I give a warning each time because it was so unusual to have visitors. Their fear was real because no one had cared to visit the facility for years. I assured them all that my visits were not for firing someone. The response was nervous chuckles. Although, after a few months it came true and I had to go to the facility to terminate an employee. So, I guess they were right in the end.

If the visits are introduced as part of leadership responsibilities, it won't be such a nerve-wracking experience for the facility staff. Let the organization know that facility visits are now leadership protocol. Communicate the purpose of the visits, what can be expected, request the local staff to prepare questions. Make visits a positive experience.

WHEELIES ARE FUN!

Safety is a core focus at any manufacturing facility. In one company, each facility tracked and publicized how many days had gone by without an accident. One late afternoon, the general manager walked to the loading dock where a forklift was sitting unattended. He proceeded to climb in and did wheelies on the loading dock. Sigh.

**Your actions are so loud I can no longer believe
what you are saying.**

The employees that were present watched the general manager as he played with the forklift. The story spread like wildfire throughout the facility. How do you recover from that? Safety focus? What safety focus?

Don't make poor choices as a leader. You may not lose your job, but you risk losing respect. Remember, leadership can be lonely. For the things that sound like fun, question if you should participate, endorse, or make any comments whatsoever.

EXPLAIN THE RULES TO ME AGAIN, PLEASE?

A frequent discussion these days is around telecommuting. One organization had a strict policy stating there was no telecommuting. The policy was communicated regularly to ensure that everyone understood the policy. It was clearly stated that the policy applied to all employees.

There was no working from home, so don't ask.... except for someone who had been telecommuting for two years before the policy was implemented. They were grandfathered in, of course. And then if a role couldn't be filled locally, it would be filled with remote employees. You know, the ones that work from their home every day. Also, if someone moves with his or her family, he or she will work remotely. That was okay. Alternatively, if someone prefers to live in a different city, then they are okay because they travel more extensively.

The policy stated no telecommuting. There was no working from home. Do not even ask. The exceptions were many. The result was employee frustration. You, can. You, cannot. You, can. You, cannot. Explain the rules to me again, please?

Whatever you say, whatever you do, as a leader you are under the microscope. Making exceptions is okay. Being fair is not being equal. Being fair to employees means recognizing individual situations and supporting solutions for them. If a company makes strong policy statements, yet has exception after exception, it just irritates everyone. Employees see who is favored by how the rules are applied. They know when the organization tries to hide or make excuses for decisions. With so many exceptions, the policy needs to reflect what the organization is willing to do. Turn the irritation into a fair practice, and the morale needle goes up.

If the organization is not willing to uphold the policy, remove it, or stop promoting it. Better yet, change it to accurately reflect the company's actual policy based on its actions. Leaders must take a reality check of their organization's policies, values, and practices. The gaps reflect poorly on the leaders. It irritates employees. It negatively impacts the culture. It creates a culture that promotes favoritism over fairness. That is not a culture that creates engaged employees.

THE LEADER BRAND

What do you want to be known for as a leader? Are you environmentally focused? Are you focused on social issues and the morality of humanity? Is your focus on building trust in your organization? Is your brand clear? Are you active within your organization and your community? Are you engaged in issues that impact more than just their company?

What is your leadership brand? What do you want it to be? How will you determine if the brand you want is the brand you are creating? Have you ever thought about your brand?

Your image is your brand. It creates an expectation for how you behave and the decisions you make. When you make decisions, those watching will say, "Yes, of course. That makes sense." Acting per your brand reinforces how others view you and determine whether they trust you. Act differently than your spoken words, and trust is gone. It is not difficult to state what you stand for.

It may be difficult to stay true to your brand when financial pressures are looming, or other leaders are pressuring for different decisions. Digging deep to find your brave heart is essential when there are external pressures. No one said leadership was going to be a cake walk.

THE CRAPPIEST JOB

Being a leader is not easy. As was shared earlier, "it is the crappiest job in the world, with moments of fulfillment. The rest of the time it is crappy. You get paid a lot of money, not because you are the best, but because you have to make difficult decisions."

Being a great leader is not always so easy, but those moments are magical when goals are celebrated, employees grow, and you are dishing out gratitude and praise. It makes all the other stuff worth it. There will be "those days" like everyone has. The difference is everyone is watching the leaders. How they deal with stress, how they deal with a crisis, all becomes a part of their brand.

Leaders make choices as we all do. The leaders' decisions are more visible and scrutinized. There is more at stake. Much more.

The role of leadership may be difficult, lonely, and challenging. But those magical moments where a leader can see their impact, it makes it all worthwhile.

NOTHING GOES UNNOTICED

Every action is observed. Every action is followed with an interpretation.

• Being followed out of the restroom by an employee who does an air fist bump. "He doesn't wash his hands. Be careful what you touch."

• Bring their lunch from home. "She is trying to eat healthier."

• Wear a wrinkled shirt. "Must have been out too late last night."

• The same consultant visits again and again. "There must be something going on between them."

The list goes on and on. Interpretations may be wrong, or they may be right. It doesn't matter. Once the words are attached to the interpretation, they are attached to the leader. Interpretation is the foundation for developing perceived reality. Some observations are funny. Some are interesting. Some are damaging. It is difficult as a leader to redirect the interpretation because most of the time, they will never know what is being said about them. And frankly, by the time the image has been formed, contradicting information will be dismissed.

CONSIDER:

• **Being a leader means being on stage all the time**. Nothing goes without observation unless it is in the privacy in your own home. Even that is open to speculation based on your behavior. Your behaviors will always be louder than your words.

• **Being a leader has moments of great joy and many more moments of hard decisions and choices that impact employees' lives**. The role of a leader is not easy. It cannot be taken lightly if you are looking to be a successful leader.

• **You create your brand**. Being intentional about your brand will define your leadership persona. Make sure it is the one you want.

• **If you want awareness on how your leadership brand is perceived, be brave, get feedback**. Don't excuse away the answers. Dig in to learn more.

• **Leadership is lonely**. Making decisions rarely results in everyone being happy. Employees may not like your choices. The company may not like your choices. It is a constant balancing act.

CHAPTER ELEVEN

FALLIBILITY IS A LEADERSHIP CONDITION

THE TRUTH IS NOT ALWAYS EASY

The bottom line is that leaders are human. They are not super humans. They are not super heroes. They are not robots. They are not immune to emotions, drives, desires, and dreams. They are absolutely, totally and wholly, human.

However, once a person takes on the title of leader, like it or not, expectations change. Visibility and watchability change. Responsibility and accountability for profoundly impacting others change. Being held to more significant standards change. The truth of the matter is:

- Leaders are held to a higher standard.
- Leaders are the company in the eyes of employees.
- Leaders have a lot of influence.
- Leaders are human first.
- Some leaders will be remembered forever because they were amazing.
- Some leaders inspire people to be better.
- Some leaders will destroy someone's confidence.
- Leaders' actions may not be reported.
- Some leaders are destructive.
- Leaders touch people's lives every day.

• Leaders' actions can cost companies, and ultimately the shareholders, millions of dollars annually for behavior that goes unchecked and not addressed.

The humanity of leaders, because they are in the leader fishbowl, is on display for everyone to see. Moreover, if everyone does not see it, they will hear about it. Word travels fast, and employees like to talk about leaders. Leaders have pressures, challenges, and troubles. They are not given a secret toolbox to take care of life riffs once they become a leader. Nope. Now those riffs are magnified in the visibility of being a leader.

Holding the role of leader does not grant good judgment. Because leaders are human, they are still going to do stupid things. Like all of us. Like you. Like me. It may not be intentional. Sometimes it is. Sometimes it may not be looking at the situation close enough, or it may be misperceiving reality. That is where awareness of perception becomes such a gift.

SHOCKING MOMENTS

The stories shared with me were from every type of leader imaginable. No rank, function, or experience level was spared in the storytelling.

There were stories of greatness, compassion, and strength. There were tragic and emotional stories. There were stories of sexual harassment and intimidation. There were stories of rape. There were stories of pornography. There were stories of affairs and families destroyed.

Then there were crazy stories like a leader going all the way to the roof of a building to urinate because he was mad and when caught, just pulled his pants up and kept "going." One leader became extremely intoxicated at a large company event. He was escorted to his hotel room to remove him from the event. He came back down on the elevator and started dancing around, this time in his briefs. Again, he was escorted to his room. Once again, he came down to the dance floor, gleefully, to keep dancing in his briefs. Again, he was escorted to his hotel room. This time he was assigned a guardian to keep him contained.

There were sad stories of drug addiction and alcoholism. There was the leader who used cocaine as though he was taking aspirin. "It's just how I deal with stuff," he said.

There was a story of a highly respected leader who was struggling from an apparent panic attack. He was watched over for almost two days by employees in a hotel room until they could get him into a treatment center. He was under watch as they feared he would hurt himself. In the end, he was discovered to be a severe alcoholic who desperately needed treatment. There were stories of suicides and mental illness.

Leaders are, more than anything else, human. Because they are leaders, they are expected to adhere to a higher standard by employees, their company, and by the community. Sometimes their behavior is just in poor taste like the leaders who dressed in offensive costumes for Halloween events.

BE OPEN

There are instances in business when things aren't right. It could be a production line problem. It could be a supplier concern. Laws, regulations, and guidelines all have an impact on business operations. There is a multitude of points that could create a bump in the road or completely kill the engine of the company. The deliverer of bad news can be on the receiving end of a leader's wrath, even when it is not their fault.

The old saying is, "Don't kill the messenger." If you shred the messenger, there is not one person that will be willing to bring anything to your attention again. That is not a good outcome. That is completely diving into a world of unnecessary risk.

SAM'S STORY

Early in his career, Sam worked in the environmental industry. Sam was wicked smart. He knew the business well. He was great at selling the product and relating to his customers. Sam's goal, like the rest of the team, was to sell as much as possible. Sam was excellent at selling because he knew the product very well. He did his homework. Sam was driven to succeed.

Sam discovered a potential long-term liability problem with the product. The problem would not be an issue immediately. However, over time, the potential lawsuits could be very costly to the company.

When Sam went to his manager, his manager went to the senior executive. The senior executive called Sam and the HR executive into his office. The dressing down began.

"You are not an engineer, are you, Sam?"

"No."

"How long have you been here, Sam?"

"Two years."

"So, Sam, you have not been here as the team developed the product, tested the product, reviewed outcomes?"

"No."

"But yet, Sam, you think you know more than anyone else here?"

Sam was discredited not only in the executive's office, but also received public floggings from both executives. The purpose was to discredit him in the event of future legal issues. Why would a company listen to someone who is not qualified to make these claims?

Let's not miss the fact that he was correct, and changes were made to the product. The idea that he had to be publicly humiliated to protect the company from the future financial loss was the chosen path. The absolute destruction of the employee who was acting with integrity was the only action the company could choose?

Leaders make choices every day. They balance the needs of the people with the needs of the organization. They adjust the inputs and the outputs. The goal is to make money. Public floggings are not necessary even if it has been advised to do so to cover potential litigation. When employees bring gaps, problems, or risks to the attention of senior leadership, consider it a gift. Thank them. Gather information. Follow up. Give the employee a response. And whether they are correct or not, thank them again. One time, the employee bringing an item to the attention of senior management may be saving the company from significant loss.

GOING, GOING, GONE

The pressure for leaders to perform is enormous. There is constant pressure to make the numbers. It never stops. When one month is over, there is another month on the horizon. When one quarter is finished, there is another quarter. That kind of continuous pressure will drive some leaders to make poor decisions. Ethics are often on the line.

Human Resources is often the function toeing the line on ethics. Ethics is the one area where decisions can quickly flip to the dark side. Pressure from line leaders to "Just let this one go. C'mon, it's their first time. I'll keep an eye on them." The second time it happens, it becomes more challenging to stick with ethics. The third time, the ethical foundation is gone.

Acting as though no one is watching leaves a high probability for derailment. Wading too much in one's ego can derail a leader. Losing humility derails leaders.

Ethics is the lighthouse for organizations. If you are unsure about what to do, revisit the ethics and value statements of the organization. It is most likely the leader already knows the answer. There is probably something that is causing them to question a decision. Don't cross the ethics line. Ask yourself how you would feel if the decision became public? How would you feel if someone you hold in high regard found out? Let that be your guidance system. Policies rarely stop anyone from doing anything.

As one brilliant leader once said, "Policies are written for those who are probably going to do it anyway." As a leader, keep your own house in order. You will have much less to worry about in the long run. It is an internal guidance system that will keep people on track.

Don't let pressure cause you to make a decision that you will regret later.

SOCIAL MEDIA AND FALSE PERSONAS

Today, these words of wisdom are shared with youth repeatedly, in the home and schools, all over the world: "Social media is forever. Just because you delete a picture does not mean it is gone forever. Your picture may already be copied. Your flip remark may be taken out of context and may already have been reshared."

Leaders listen up. These are great words of wisdom shared with youth that you should adopt, too.

Your email, your memos, your text messages, your messenger comments, meetings, and any other communication venue are all vulnerable.

Everyone should mind his or her Ps & Qs with social media. As mentioned earlier, leaders are on stage all the time. Use privacy settings to keep social media solely for friends and family if need be. Also, remember work friends are great until they get upset with you. Always bear in mind that wherever you post personal information, and employees and co-workers have access, any of your personal information is easily shared within the workplace. Social media can be used against you.

Sandy was hired as a leader and came with incredible credentials. She had a pedigree education. Extensive experience at Fortune 100 companies. Her knowledge and expertise were exactly what the company needed. When she arrived for her first day of work, she was greeted with enthusiastic handshakes and welcoming gestures. The team needed a strong leader. Her peers were excited to have her join the team. Joy was in the air.

The first few weeks were spent getting to know the team members, operations, and peers. She was enthusiastically jumping in with all she had. About two months in, her reporting team began to have some concerns. Sandy did not know the basics of the function, not even the terminology. Her experience was reported to be vast with huge projects under her belt. How could she possibly not know the basics of the function? Something was off.

Team members began to talk to each other over the lunch table.

"I asked her about her time at University. She used the wrong city name."

"I asked her about her last company, she got the CEO name wrong, and he has been there for five years."

"I was talking to her about our last project. She did not have a clue what I was talking about."

The team went to task and started digging. They started with social media. Facebook posts. Instagram posts. LinkedIn profile. They researched friends and connections. They were regular investigators. They dug into her stated education and degrees. Flags were raised all over the place. They spent two months looking into her information.

In the meantime, her demeanor changed abruptly. Instead of the engaging new leader, she became defensive and angry at any talk of her history. When she was pressed to answer questions about the function, she would turn on the employee, chastising them for bringing up topics that do not need discussion.

Peers were having some concerns during this time, but attributed the behavior to being new. After all, she was fun to be around and fit in well. Her immediate manager liked her. She was full of enthusiasm. She struggled to answer questions about the business but again, she was new, and their company was complex.

The employees developed their plan. They wanted to carefully present their findings. Their accusations had to be backed up with reliable information. One day they made their move and met with the HR leader. They provided all their data and findings. The verification process of the information did not take long. Their investigative work paid off.

Everything on Sandy's resume was false. The references were fake. It was one big game for Sandy. She was immediately released. However, the damage was done. The business had suffered. Employees had suffered. Thanks to social media and treating it as though no one was watching, the real Sandy was revealed.

Whatever you say on social media, whatever you do, never act as though no one is watching. They are watching.

TITLES DO NOT ENTITLE

It was a great day to head over to the local coffee shop and do some writing. I walked towards the counter and stood behind the one man in front of me. At first, I thought he was an irate customer. Perhaps his coffee drink was wrong? I listened in because frankly, it was hard not to hear what he was saying so loudly and sarcastically.

"The donuts were not sealed very well last night. Today they were all dry. You were here last night. You need to pay better attention. If you want to work here, you gotta pay attention. There are lots of people who want to work here. You better get it together. I want the floors cleaned. I mean I want them clean, not like last night." It was the manager speaking.

I looked at the young man behind the counter. His facial expression was a mix of disgust, disbelief, irritation, and frustration. The young man looked at me, knowing that I heard everything. I looked him in the eyes.

The manager turned to see me standing there. He said, "Oh, hi," and smiled at me. He turned back to the employee and kept on with his instructions and demeaning words. I stood there and watched him. After about five minutes he turned and said, "I'm sorry. I have to go so I have to tell him these things."

I could not help myself. I replied, "Oh no, don't mind me. I am only a customer just waiting to purchase a coffee. Please continue chastising your employee in front of the entire place. You are doing a great job at that."

The young man smirked. The manager looked confused and left. I walked up to the counter to order my coffee. The young man was apologetic for my wait and for having to hear all of what just transpired. At least the employee understood customer service, decency, and respect.

A title does not entitle. It does not empower leaders to berate others and behave in such a way that negatively impacts the individual nor the perception of the company.

THE VISITORS

Executive visits can be energizing, uplifting, and inspiring. The opportunity to speak to a senior leader of a company is a big deal for an employee. It has meaning. It makes them feel as though they matter to the company. Leaders are agents of their company. Leaders are the company.

In very large companies, senior executive visits are sporadic. When they are scheduled to visit, the entire store is mobilized to receive them. The preparation takes several weeks. If it was run the way it should be, they should not have to prepare before a visit you say? Don't you clean your house before a party? Don't you do special preparations before family arrives for holidays? It is what we do. The extra touch. The extra effort. Business or personal. We want to make a good impression.

When a senior leader walks in the door, all eyes are on them. One such visit became memorable for one store manager, and the surrounding employees and customers.

While berating the store manager for noticing fruit flies above one section of fruit, the senior leader was determined to be dramatic. He grabbed a shopping cart and slammed it into the wall. He then picked up a piece of fruit and said, "Give me $5 if I make this." He then proceeded to lob the fruit towards the garbage can that was about 20 feet away. He continued his show by stating, "If I had more time, I would line up all the employees and require them to throw out every piece of fruit in the store."

Maybe not the best marketing technique for the customers walking through the store? The total lack of awareness of how his behavior was impacting every constituent group in the store is an example of behaving for the leader's own ego. Executives are paid to lead their organization so that profits are optimized, and losses are minimized. They are expected to live by the company's values and policies. They are the role models for the organization. Upholding that responsibility is an everyday affair.

Another store manager had a challenging day when the visiting executive stated in the middle of the store, surrounded by employees and customers, "This is the dirtiest store I have ever seen. Why is this store kept open? The cleanliness is terrible." In front of customers. In front of employees. Why not take the conversation to a back room?

Word gets out when these incidents transpire. The executive may be thinking that the word getting out is a great strategy to let others know to up their game. The real outcome is the respect for that leader is diminished, if not completely destroyed. Customers are offended. Employees are mortified. Basic respect and decency are required to be any leader. It takes compassion and humility to be a great leader.

Leaders are human beings. They make mistakes. Providing a title does not change that basic fact.

However, leaders make choices. They make choices how they treat others. At the end of the day, it is more than a leader speaking to an employee. It is a human speaking to fellow human being.

CONSIDER:

• **Even though leaders are human, they are held to a higher standard**. Because they have chosen leadership as a profession does not mean all their traits and challenges change. They are still human, they also now lead.

• **A title does not create entitlement**. You can't treat people as though they are inferior or subservient. Now is the time to be more caring. More engaging. Be humbler.

• **Take it off the floor.** Period. Save your words for when it is appropriate.

• **Respect others**.

CHAPTER TWELVE

PLAN FOR THE UNEXPECTED

CAPITAL 'S' AND A RED HIGH-HEELED SHOE

The executive stood in front of the room by the podium. This town hall was his opportunity to openly share critical messages. It was important to him that he was fully understood. He loved the idea of transparency. It was one of his core leadership beliefs.

The company itself was in the middle of a few significant changes. One business was being sold. One business was being purchased. As a leader, he was most pleased that the employees in the business being sold would retain their jobs. These changes were challenging enough, but it was much harder if people were going to lose their jobs. It was more difficult to walk in the door and look at them each day, pretending as though everything was status quo. This time, he knew they would all transfer to the purchasing company. It felt good.

There were several internal projects that everyone knew about, and he knew from the emails he had been receiving that his employees needed an update. He was also excited because there were several of his employees that were going to be recognized for some great work they had done. He was one to lavish praise, and he always meant it. The town hall plan was set.

He began the town hall sharing the updates on the company's financials. He then proceeded to share internal project updates. While he was speaking, he decided to fill everyone in on the business being sold and make sure that everyone knew they were going to be transferring to the new company. Minimizing any concerns or fear was important for this leader.

He shared detailed information about the business about to be sold. It was a strategic move that would allow the company to align its core business. It made sense. The employees gasped and looked around at each other. This was news to all the employees.

The HR executive in the room quickly sat up in her chair. She pulled out her phone to text one of the business leaders.

"O.M.G. Capital S, Red High Heel Shoe, Asterisk, Exclamation Point. Did he just say that?"

The VP responded. "Yep. We have a problem."

The business that was to be sold was still in negotiations. It was a confidential transaction. Legal was completing reviews. The executive exquisitely shared details, time frames, and more for a deal that was confidential and yet to be finalized.

It's a true story.

Leaders make mistakes. But there should always be a plan.

What are the first three steps that need to be taken if something goes awry? The whole process does not need to be detailed, but those first three steps need to be clear. Like a fire drill in school, leaders need to have a plan.

Instead of spending the first few moments wondering what to do, know what to do. Knowing the first few steps moves you in the right direction and gives the main players time to assess the damage and determine next steps.

In this case, the steps looked like this:

1. Call the CEO.

2. Call the legal department.

3. Call the head of the business being sold.

Always expect the unexpected. Companies are full of leaders and leaders are human. Mistakes are going to be made. Make sure there is a plan in place. Prepare like first responders, they always know what their first steps are in any situation. Hopefully you will never need the plan, but it is great to have available, just in case.

CONSIDER:

• **"What if?"** What if word gets out? What if rumors begin? What if they are true? What if they are false? Add these questions to your toolbox.

• **Have a plan**. Make sure everyone knows what the first three steps are if something goes wrong. Easily said. Not so often done.

CHAPTER THIRTEEN

THE FINAL SAY

THE MULTIFACETED LENS

This book was written to share the views on leadership through the HR lens. HR has a multifaceted perspective on leaders. They hear and see input from employees, managers, peers, other HR leaders, and from the leader themselves. They view all. That is the value of looking at leadership through the eyes of HR. They have a perspective that is holistic and significant.

Some of the outcomes of the interviews surprised me. Some amazed me. Some observations were jaw-dropping. They were always fascinating. I did discover that through the HR lens, there were distinct views on leadership. The lessons are essential for leaders, for those who want to be leaders, and for human resource professionals to know and consider as they support leaders.

In a nutshell, the outcomes looked like this:

• **The most influential leader for any person in their career may very well be their first leader**. If you are the leader of an employee new to the workforce, be keenly aware of the influence you have on them.

• **No one could have predicted the accelerated rapid change and the number of changes currently in the world**. No one predicted the impact these changes would have on personal lives. That impact on individual lives carries itself into the workplace every day. It has created a new challenge for leaders as they struggle to keep employees present. It is only going to be more significant as new technology emerges.

• **The number one characteristic identified as important for any leader was humility**. There were five in total: humility, decision-making, the strength to say no, communication, and trust. There was no question that humility was number one.

• **It will take time but find your style as a leader**. Trying to emulate a great leader only means you are not comfortable with yourself. That is where you should focus your time and attention.

• **Every leader has trigger points that take them off center**. Know what they are and work to get them under control. The first step is to be aware of them. On the flip side, leaders have the ability to impact employee messaging with their leadership platform. Be mindful of what is being said.

• **Make sure as the leader, actions align with the company values**. If not, there will be a negative impact on the culture. Also, know that what leaders see as the culture from their vantage point, may not be what the rest of the organization is experiencing. Get out of the office, visit other locations, meet people.

• **New leaders have great opportunities**. The first thing to learn is how to manage. Next, get comfortable with getting your lollipops from different sources. Remember it is a journey that requires immersion into the experience.

• **Leaders are stewards of the people**. Respect them and treat everyone as if they matter because they do. Every person matters. A title does not make a leader more important than others. A title means the decisions are harder and impact others more significantly.

• **Leaders are onstage every day**. Mind your Ps and Qs. If you think no one is watching, think again. Everything you touch, write, speak, share, is discoverable. And because you are a leader, it now becomes much more interesting to others.

• **Above all, leaders are human**. They make terrible mistakes and sometimes have poor judgment. Because they are leaders, they are held to higher standards. They have emotions, dreams, desires, and goals. They feel pressure and deal with the same internal struggles as those that do not have the title of leader.

• **You never know what can go wrong**. Always have a plan for what may go wrong. It does not need to be a fancy detailed plan, just a simple plan will do.

FINAL THOUGHTS

Being a leader is a fantastic opportunity and a huge responsibility. It is a dream come true for so many.

The stories shared by those interviewed were intriguing, inspiring, frightening and entertaining. The most astounding outcome was the incredible alignment of the messages they shared.

When all was said and done, I walked away with the feeling that the future of leadership holds much hope with attention, focus, education, and coaching. Leaders, new and experienced, need time to catch their breath. They need time to step away from everyday pressures to learn, get coaching, regroup, and apply new learnings.

I believe the leader that is an intentional tyrant is more rare than ordinary. Some truly are. Most are not. Being ill-equipped and lacking appropriate feedback results in adverse behavior. The incredible pace of change and the need to put people in leadership positions in fast-paced growth situations is the more significant challenge. Leaders need support and coaching to be successful. Leaders are not equipped to deal with the constant rapid change around them. Yet leaders are expected to show the way, ease the burden, and make the journey successful for all.

Everyone has a view on leadership. Is their view correct? Who knows? If they think it is correct, it is correct. It is the game of perception. The years of experience represented in this book provides some terrific insight into how leaders become great, how they derail, and specific areas of focus to develop successful leaders.

The most important lesson is that leaders are human. When given the title of leader, there isn't much room for error. Leaders are not given much grace for making mistakes. They are expected to know better, to behave better than the average person. People are going to talk about what leaders do, or don't do, now and for years to come.

What do you want them to say about you?

Leadership is an incredible adventure for those willing to take it all on. Whatever you do, enjoy the experience, and make it joyful for those around you. So, grab a stack of index cards, get curious about your new lollipops, and prepare for the ride.

ACKNOWLEDGMENTS

To Rod. The man who suggested I write a book. He thought it would be interesting to write about HR stories and thought I would be the perfect person to author the book. So here it is, Rod!

To Steve, who has been a friend and inspiration since the day I met him. He taught me that working hard is great but having fun along the way is the cherry on top. Laugh, smile, and enjoy the experience.

Thanks to Tim, who took a chance and invited me onto the team to help build a corporate university from the ground up. I did not have a clue what was ahead of me, but it was nothing less than great.

And Phil, who has supported me in so many ways.

And to Paula, always willing to share ideas that move me forward towards my goals. You are a gift.

To every human resource professional who shared their experiences with such honesty and passion, thank you. You have shared a great gift with your stories so that others can learn from all your experience.

ABOUT THE AUTHOR

Barbara is a speaker, author, leadership coach, podcaster, entrepreneur, and mom. She has spent her life challenging rules and bad advice that hold people back from achieving their greatness. She loves to share knowledge, ideas, and inspire others to find their joy.

She believes life is an adventure and adventures don't happen by sitting on a couch. She loves her family, dogs, photography, nature, travel, learning, creating aha moments for others, and lacinato kale.

Life is made up of moments and every moment matters. Make them great moments.

Look for "Barbara Inspires" on Twitter, Instagram, Facebook, Podbean, Stitcher, and iTunes.

You can visit Barbara at her website:
barbarawichman.com

To request Barbara for speaking engagements and workshops:
barbara@barbarawichman.com

Barbara WICHMAN

www.ingramcontent.com/pod-product-compliance
Lightning Source LLC
Chambersburg PA
CBHW031938190326
41519CB00007B/580